Cram101 Textbook Outlines to accompany:

Sport Psychology: Concepts and Applications

Cox, 5th Edition

An Academic Internet Publishers (AIPI) publication (c) 2007.

You have a discounted membership at www.Cram101.com with this book.

Get all of the practice tests for the chapters of this textbook, and access in-depth reference material for writing essays and papers. Here is an example from a Cram101 Biology text:

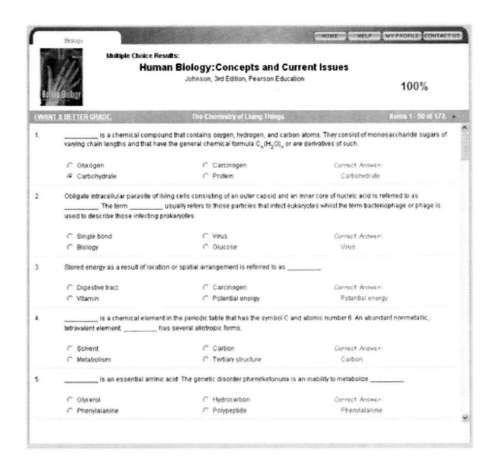

When you need problem solving help with math, stats, and other disciplines, www.Cram101.com will walk through the formulas and solutions step by step.

With Cram101.com online, you also have access to extensive reference material.

You will nail those essays and papers. Here is an example from a Cram101 Biology text:

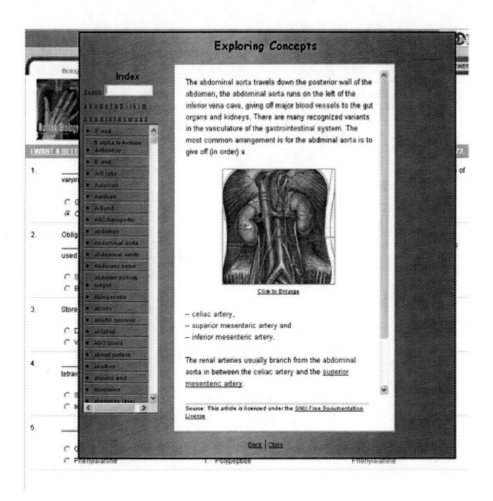

Visit **www.Cram101.com**, click Sign Up at the top of the screen, and enter DK73DW in the promo code box on the registration screen. Access to www.Cram101.com is normally $9.95, but because you have purchased this book, your access fee is only $4.95. Sign up and stop highlighting textbooks forever.

Learning System

Cram101 Textbook Outlines is a learning system. The notes in this book are the highlights of your textbook, you will never have to highlight a book again.

How to use this book. Take this book to class, it is your notebook for the lecture. The notes and highlights on the left hand side of the pages follow the outline and order of the textbook. All you have to do is follow along while your intructor presents the lecture. Circle the items emphasized in class and add other important information on the right side. With Cram101 Textbook Outlines you'll spend less time writing and more time listening. Learning becomes more efficient.

Cram101.com Online

Increase your studying efficiency by using Cram101.com's practice tests and online reference material. It is the perfect complement to Cram101 Textbook Outlines. Use self-teaching matching tests or simulate in-class testing with comprehensive multiple choice tests, or simply use Cram's true and false tests for quick review. Cram101.com even allows you to enter your in-class notes for an integrated studying format combining the textbook notes with your class notes.

Sport Psychology: Concepts and Applications
Cox, 5th

CONTENTS

Motivation	In psychology, motivation is the driving force (desire) behind all actions of an organism.
Attitude	An enduring mental representation of a person, place, or thing that evokes an emotional response and related behavior is called attitude.
Enrichment	Deliberately making an environment more novel, complex, and perceptually or intellectually stimulating is referred to as enrichment.
Social facilitation	Social facilitation refers to the process by which a person's performance is increased when other members of a group engage in similar behavior.
Physiology	The study of the functions and activities of living cells, tissues, and organs and of the physical and chemical phenomena involved is referred to as physiology.
Learning	Learning is a relatively permanent change in behavior that results from experience. Thus, to attribute a behavioral change to learning, the change must be relatively permanent and must result from experience.
Laboratory setting	Research setting in which the behavior of interest does not naturally occur is called a laboratory setting.
Social psychology	Social psychology is the study of the nature and causes of human social behavior, with an emphasis on how people think towards each other and how they relate to each other.
Hypnosis	Hypnosis is a psychological state whose existence and effects are strongly debated. Some believe that it is a state under which the subject's mind becomes so suggestible that the hypnotist, the one who induces the state, can establish communication with the subconscious mind of the subject and command behavior that the subject would not choose to perform in a conscious state.
Anxiety	Anxiety is a complex combination of the feeling of fear, apprehension and worry often accompanied by physical sensations such as palpitations, chest pain and/or shortness of breath.
Zajonc	Zajonc is best known for his decades of work on the mere exposure effect, the phenomenon that repeated exposure to a stimulus brings about an attitude change in relation to the stimulus.
Personality	Personality refers to the pattern of enduring characteristics that differentiates a person, the patterns of behaviors that make each individual unique.
Society	The social sciences use the term society to mean a group of people that form a semi-closed (or semi-open) social system, in which most interactions are with other individuals belonging to the group.
Clinician	A health professional authorized to provide services to people suffering from one or more pathologies is a clinician.
Personality disorder	A mental disorder characterized by a set of inflexible, maladaptive personality traits that keep a person from functioning properly in society is referred to as a personality disorder.
Affect	A subjective feeling or emotional tone often accompanied by bodily expressions noticeable to others is called affect.
Clinical psychology	Clinical psychology is involved in the diagnosis, assessment, and treatment of patients with mental or behavioral disorders, and conducts research in these various areas.
Knowledge base	The general background information a person possesses, which influences most cognitive task performance is called the knowledge base.
Theories	Theories are logically self-consistent models or frameworks describing the behavior of a certain natural or social phenomenon. They are broad explanations and predictions concerning phenomena of interest.

Go to Cram101.com for the Practice Tests for this Chapter.

Motivation	In psychology, motivation is the driving force (desire) behind all actions of an organism.
Innate	Innate behavior is not learned or influenced by the environment, rather, it is present or predisposed at birth.
Drive reduction	Drive reduction theories are based on the need-state. Drive activates behavior. Reinforcement occurs whenever drive is reduced, leading to learning of whatever response solves the need. Thus the reduction in need serves as reinforcement and produces reinforcement of the response that leads to it.
Drive Theory	Drive Theory states that due to the unpredictable nature of people, a person performing a task rarely knows for certain what others are going to do in response. This creates a state of arousal that in some cases will facilitate performance, while in other cases it will inhibit performance.
Insight	Insight refers to a sudden awareness of the relationships among various elements that had previously appeared to be independent of one another.
Maslow	Maslow is mostly noted today for his proposal of a hierarchy of human needs which he often presented as a pyramid. Maslow was an instrumental player in the formation of the humanistic movement, also known as the third force in psychology.
Attention	Attention is the cognitive process of selectively concentrating on one thing while ignoring other things. Psychologists have labeled three types of attention: sustained attention, selective attention, and divided attention.
Hierarchy of needs	Maslow's hierarchy of needs is often depicted as a pyramid consisting of five levels: the four lower levels are grouped together as deficiency needs, while the top level is termed being needs. While our deficiency needs must be met, our being needs are continually shaping our behavior.
McClelland	McClelland asserts that human motivation comprises three dominant needs: the need for achievement (N-Ach), the need for power (N-Pow) and the need for affiliation (N-Affil). The subjective importance of each need varies from individual to individual and depends also on an individual's cultural background.
Theories	Theories are logically self-consistent models or frameworks describing the behavior of a certain natural or social phenomenon. They are broad explanations and predictions concerning phenomena of interest.
Spence	Spence attributed improvement in performance to motivational factors rather than habit factors. His Discrimination Learning Theory argued that reinforcement combined with frustration or inhibitors facilitates finding a correct stimulus among a cluster which includes incorrect ones.
Hull	Hull is best known for the Drive Reduction Theory which postulated that behavior occurs in response to primary drives such as hunger, thirst, sexual interest, etc. When the goal of the drive is attained the drive is reduced. This reduction of drive serves as a reinforcer for learning.
Construct	A generalized concept, such as anxiety or gravity, is a construct.
Intrinsic motivation	Intrinsic motivation causes people to engage in an activity for its own sake. They are subjective factors and include self-determination, curiosity, challenge, effort, and others.
Personality trait	According to the Diagnostic and Statistical Manual of the American Psychiatric Association, a personality trait is a "prominent aspect of personality that is exhibited in a wide range of important social and personal contexts. ...".
Personality	Personality refers to the pattern of enduring characteristics that differentiates a person,

Go to **Cram101.com** for the Practice Tests for this Chapter.

the patterns of behaviors that make each individual unique.

Trait	An enduring personality characteristic that tends to lead to certain behaviors is called a trait. The term trait also means a genetically inherited feature of an organism.
Self-efficacy	Self-efficacy is the belief that one has the capabilities to execute the courses of actions required to manage prospective situations.
Bandura	Bandura is best known for his work on social learning theory or Social Cognitivism. His famous Bobo doll experiment illustrated that people learn from observing others.
Social cognitive theory	Social cognitive theory defines human behavior as a triadic, dynamic, and reciprocal interaction of personal factors, behavior, and the environment. Response consequences of a behavior are used to form expectations of behavioral outcomes. It is the ability to form these expectations that give humans the capability to predict the outcomes of their behavior, before the behavior is performed.
Learning	Learning is a relatively permanent change in behavior that results from experience. Thus, to attribute a behavioral change to learning, the change must be relatively permanent and must result from experience.
Modeling	A type of behavior learned through observation of others demonstrating the same behavior is modeling.
Achievement motivation	The psychological need in humans for success is called achievement motivation.
Perception	Perception is the process of acquiring, interpreting, selecting, and organizing sensory information.
Affect	A subjective feeling or emotional tone often accompanied by bodily expressions noticeable to others is called affect.
Anxiety	Anxiety is a complex combination of the feeling of fear, apprehension and worry often accompanied by physical sensations such as palpitations, chest pain and/or shortness of breath.
Positive feedback	When a change in a variable occurs in a system, the system responds. In the case of positive feedback the response of the system is to cause that variable to increase in the same direction.
Feedback	Feedback refers to information returned to a person about the effects a response has had.
Friendship	The essentials of friendship are reciprocity and commitment between individuals who see themselves more or less as equals. Interaction between friends rests on a more equal power base than the interaction between children and adults.
Variable	A variable refers to a measurable factor, characteristic, or attribute of an individual or a system.
Attitude	An enduring mental representation of a person, place, or thing that evokes an emotional response and related behavior is called attitude.
Acquisition	Acquisition is the process of adapting to the environment, learning or becoming conditioned. In classical conditoning terms, it is the initial learning of the stimulus response link, which involves a neutral stimulus being associated with a unconditioned stimulus and becoming a conditioned stimulus.
Habit	A habit is a response that has become completely separated from its eliciting stimulus. Early learning theorists used the term to describe S-R associations, however not all S-R associations become a habit, rather many are extinguished after reinforcement is withdrawn.

Physiology	The study of the functions and activities of living cells, tissues, and organs and of the physical and chemical phenomena involved is referred to as physiology.
Cognition	The intellectual processes through which information is obtained, transformed, stored, retrieved, and otherwise used is cognition.
Antecedents	In behavior modification, events that typically precede the target response are called antecedents.
Moderator variable	A variable that affects the relation between two other variables is called the moderator variable.
Laboratory setting	Research setting in which the behavior of interest does not naturally occur is called a laboratory setting.
Social comparison	Social comparison theory is the idea that individuals learn about and assess themselves by comparison with other people. Research shows that individuals tend to lean more toward social comparisons in situations that are ambiguous.
Meta-analysis	In statistics, a meta-analysis combines the results of several studies that address a set of related research hypotheses.
Hypothesis	A specific statement about behavior or mental processes that is testable through research is a hypothesis.

Motivation	In psychology, motivation is the driving force (desire) behind all actions of an organism.
Achievement motivation	The psychological need in humans for success is called achievement motivation.
Self-efficacy	Self-efficacy is the belief that one has the capabilities to execute the courses of actions required to manage prospective situations.
Bandura	Bandura is best known for his work on social learning theory or Social Cognitivism. His famous Bobo doll experiment illustrated that people learn from observing others.
Cognitive restructuring	Cognitive restructuring refers to any behavior therapy procedure that attempts to alter the manner in which a client thinks about life so that he or she changes overt behavior and emotions.
Developmental level	An individual's current state of physical, emotional, and intellectual development is called the developmental level.
Learning	Learning is a relatively permanent change in behavior that results from experience. Thus, to attribute a behavioral change to learning, the change must be relatively permanent and must result from experience.
Social comparison	Social comparison theory is the idea that individuals learn about and assess themselves by comparison with other people. Research shows that individuals tend to lean more toward social comparisons in situations that are ambiguous.
Ego	In Freud's view the Ego serves to balance our primitive needs and our moral beliefs and taboos. Relying on experience, a healthy Ego provides the ability to adapt to reality and interact with the outside world.
Mastery orientation	According to Dweck, mastery orientation is an outlook in which individuals focus on the task rather than on their ability, have positive affect, and generate solution-oriented strategies that improve their performance.
Personality trait	According to the Diagnostic and Statistical Manual of the American Psychiatric Association, a personality trait is a "prominent aspect of personality that is exhibited in a wide range of important social and personal contexts. ...".
Personality	Personality refers to the pattern of enduring characteristics that differentiates a person, the patterns of behaviors that make each individual unique.
Trait	An enduring personality characteristic that tends to lead to certain behaviors is called a trait. The term trait also means a genetically inherited feature of an organism.
Anxiety	Anxiety is a complex combination of the feeling of fear, apprehension and worry often accompanied by physical sensations such as palpitations, chest pain and/or shortness of breath.
Questionnaire	A self-report method of data collection or clinical assessment method in which the individual being studied checks off items on a printed list, answers multiple-choice questions, or writes out answers to essay questions aimed at producing a selfdescription is called questionnaire.
Perception	Perception is the process of acquiring, interpreting, selecting, and organizing sensory information.
Positive reinforcement	In positive reinforcement, a stimulus is added and the rate of responding increases.
Reinforcement	In operant conditioning, reinforcement is any change in an environment that (a) occurs after the behavior, (b) seems to make that behavior re-occur more often in the future and (c) that

Go to **Cram101.com** for the Practice Tests for this Chapter.

reoccurence of behavior must be the result of the change.

Attention	Attention is the cognitive process of selectively concentrating on one thing while ignoring other things. Psychologists have labeled three types of attention: sustained attention, selective attention, and divided attention.
Intrinsic motivation	Intrinsic motivation causes people to engage in an activity for its own sake. They are subjective factors and include self-determination, curiosity, challenge, effort, and others.
Cooperative learning	Cooperative learning was proposed in response to traditional curriculum-driven education. In cooperative learning environments, students interact in purposively structured heterogenous group to support the learning of one self and others in the same group.
Affect	A subjective feeling or emotional tone often accompanied by bodily expressions noticeable to others is called affect.
Construct	A generalized concept, such as anxiety or gravity, is a construct.
Median	The median is a number that separates the higher half of a sample, a population, or a probability distribution from the lower half. It is the middle value in a distribution, above and below which lie an equal number of values.
Attitude	An enduring mental representation of a person, place, or thing that evokes an emotional response and related behavior is called attitude.
Hypothesis	A specific statement about behavior or mental processes that is testable through research is a hypothesis.
Matching hypothesis	The matching hypothesis is a popular theory proposed by Walster in 1966, on what causes people to be attracted to their partners. It claims that people are more likely to form long term relationships with people who are roughly equally as physically attractive as themselves.
Negative feedback	In negative feedback, the output of a system is added back into the input, so as to reverse the direction of change. This tends to keep the output from changing, so it is stabilizing and attempts to maintain homeostasis.
Self-esteem	Self-esteem refers to a person's subjective appraisal of himself or herself as intrinsically positive or negative to some degree.
Feedback	Feedback refers to information returned to a person about the effects a response has had.
Predisposition	Predisposition refers to an inclination or diathesis to respond in a certain way, either inborn or acquired. In abnormal psychology, it is a factor that lowers the ability to withstand stress and inclines the individual toward pathology.
Maladaptive	In psychology, a behavior or trait is adaptive when it helps an individual adjust and function well within their social environment. A maladaptive behavior or trait is counterproductive to the individual.

Go to **Cram101.com** for the Practice Tests for this Chapter.

Attribution theory	Attribution theory is concerned with the ways in which people explain the behavior of others. It explores how individuals "attribute" causes to events and how this cognitive perception affects their motivation.
Motivation	In psychology, motivation is the driving force (desire) behind all actions of an organism.
Perception	Perception is the process of acquiring, interpreting, selecting, and organizing sensory information.
Ego	In Freud's view the Ego serves to balance our primitive needs and our moral beliefs and taboos. Relying on experience, a healthy Ego provides the ability to adapt to reality and interact with the outside world.
Self-esteem	Self-esteem refers to a person's subjective appraisal of himself or herself as intrinsically positive or negative to some degree.
Cognitive approach	A cognitive approach focuses on the mental processes involved in knowing: how we direct our attention, perceive, remember, think, and solve problems.
Fritz Heider	Attribution theory in social psychology was initiated by Fritz Heider in 1958. It concerned how people choose explanations for the behavior of others. It explores how individuals attribute causes to events and how this cognitive perception affects their motivation.
Innate	Innate behavior is not learned or influenced by the environment, rather, it is present or predisposed at birth.
Wisdom	Wisdom is the ability to make correct judgments and decisions. It is an intangible quality gained through experience. Whether or not something is wise is determined in a pragmatic sense by its popularity, how long it has been around, and its ability to predict against future events.
Causation	Causation concerns the time order relationship between two or more objects such that if a specific antecendent condition occurs the same consequent must always follow.
Locus of control	The place to which an individual attributes control over the receiving of reinforcers -either inside or outside the self is referred to as locus of control.
Scheme	According to Piaget, a hypothetical mental structure that permits the classification and organization of new information is called a scheme.
Construct	A generalized concept, such as anxiety or gravity, is a construct.
Psychometric	Psychometric study is concerned with the theory and technique of psychological measurement, which includes the measurement of knowledge, abilities, attitudes, and personality traits. The field is primarily concerned with the study of differences between individuals
Socialization	Social rules and social relations are created, communicated, and changed in verbal and nonverbal ways creating social complexity useful in identifying outsiders and intelligent breeding partners. The process of learning these skills is called socialization.
Affect	A subjective feeling or emotional tone often accompanied by bodily expressions noticeable to others is called affect.
Ethnicity	Ethnicity refers to a characteristic based on cultural heritage, nationality characteristics, race, religion, and language.
External attributions	External attributions are those causes of behavior believed to be situational demands and environmental constraints.
Rotter	Rotter focused on the application of social learning theory (SLT) to clinical psychology. She introduced the ideas of learning from generalized expectancies of reinforcement and internal/external locus of control (self-initiated change versus change influenced by others).

Go to **Cram101.com** for the Practice Tests for this Chapter.

	According to Rotter, health outcomes could be improved by the development of a sense of personal control over one's life.
Internal attributions	Internal attributions occur when an individual ascribes the causes of behavior to personal dispositions, traits, abilities, and feelings.
Cognition	The intellectual processes through which information is obtained, transformed, stored, retrieved, and otherwise used is cognition.
Emotion	An emotion is a mental states that arise spontaneously, rather than through conscious effort. They are often accompanied by physiological changes.
Affective	Affective is the way people react emotionally, their ability to feel another living thing's pain or joy.
Guilt	Guilt describes many concepts related to a negative emotion or condition caused by actions which are believed to be, morally wrong. According to Freud, the avoidance of guilt is the basis for moral behavior.
Depression	In everyday language depression refers to any downturn in mood, which may be relatively transitory and perhaps due to something trivial. This is differentiated from Clinical depression which is marked by symptoms that last two weeks or more and are so severe that they interfere with daily living.
Learned helplessness	Learned helplessness is a description of the effect of inescapable positive punishment (such as electrical shock) on animal (and by extension, human) behavior.
Immune system	The most important function of the human immune system occurs at the cellular level of the blood and tissues. The lymphatic and blood circulation systems are highways for specialized white blood cells. These cells include B cells, T cells, natural killer cells, and macrophages. All function with the primary objective of recognizing, attacking and destroying bacteria, viruses, cancer cells, and all substances seen as foreign.
Self-efficacy	Self-efficacy is the belief that one has the capabilities to execute the courses of actions required to manage prospective situations.
Deprivation	Deprivation, is the loss or withholding of normal stimulation, nutrition, comfort, love, and so forth; a condition of lacking. The level of stimulation is less than what is required.
Maladaptive	In psychology, a behavior or trait is adaptive when it helps an individual adjust and function well within their social environment. A maladaptive behavior or trait is counterproductive to the individual.
Adaptation	Adaptation is a lowering of sensitivity to a stimulus following prolonged exposure to that stimulus. Behavioral adaptations are special ways a particular organism behaves to survive in its natural habitat.
Script	A schema, or behavioral sequence, for an event is called a script. It is a form of schematic organization, with real-world events organized in terms of temporal and causal relations between component acts.
Attention	Attention is the cognitive process of selectively concentrating on one thing while ignoring other things. Psychologists have labeled three types of attention: sustained attention, selective attention, and divided attention.
Egocentrism	The inability to distinguish between one's own perspective and someone else's is referred to as egocentrism.
Hypothesis	A specific statement about behavior or mental processes that is testable through research is a hypothesis.

Go to **Cram101.com** for the Practice Tests for this Chapter.

Self-serving bias	A self-serving bias is the tendency to view one's successes as stemming from internal factors and one's failures as stemming from external factors.
Shaping	The concept of reinforcing successive, increasingly accurate approximations to a target behavior is called shaping. The target behavior is broken down into a hierarchy of elemental steps, each step more sophisticated then the last. By successively reinforcing each of the the elemental steps, a form of differential reinforcement, until that step is learned while extinguishing the step below, the target behavior is gradually achieved.

18

Go to **Cram101.com** for the Practice Tests for this Chapter.

Intrinsic motivation	Intrinsic motivation causes people to engage in an activity for its own sake. They are subjective factors and include self-determination, curiosity, challenge, effort, and others.
Extrinsic motivation	Responding to external incentives such as rewards and punishments is form of extrinsic motivation. Traditionally, extrinsic motivation has been used to motivate employees: Payments, rewards, control, or punishments.
Motivation	In psychology, motivation is the driving force (desire) behind all actions of an organism.
Pitch	Pitch is the psychological interpretation of a sound or musical tone corresponding to its physical frequency
Construct	A generalized concept, such as anxiety or gravity, is a construct.
Autonomy	Autonomy is the condition of something that does not depend on anything else.
Positive feedback	When a change in a variable occurs in a system, the system responds. In the case of positive feedback the response of the system is to cause that variable to increase in the same direction.
Negative feedback	In negative feedback, the output of a system is added back into the input, so as to reverse the direction of change. This tends to keep the output from changing, so it is stabilizing and attempts to maintain homeostasis.
Feedback	Feedback refers to information returned to a person about the effects a response has had.
Perception	Perception is the process of acquiring, interpreting, selecting, and organizing sensory information.
Ego	In Freud's view the Ego serves to balance our primitive needs and our moral beliefs and taboos. Relying on experience, a healthy Ego provides the ability to adapt to reality and interact with the outside world.
Innate	Innate behavior is not learned or influenced by the environment, rather, it is present or predisposed at birth.
Sufficient condition	To say that A is a sufficient condition for B is to say precisely the converse: that A cannot occur without B, or whenever A occurs, B occurs. That there is a fire is sufficient for there being smoke.
Stages	Stages represent relatively discrete periods of time in which functioning is qualitatively different from functioning at other periods.
Sensation	Sensation is the first stage in the chain of biochemical and neurologic events that begins with the impinging of a stimulus upon the receptor cells of a sensory organ, which then leads to perception, the mental state that is reflected in statements like "I see a uniformly blue wall."
Punishment	Punishment is the addtion of a stimulus that reduces the frequency of a response, or the removal of a stimulus that results in a reduction of the response.
Internalization	The developmental change from behavior that is externally controlled to behavior that is controlled by internal standards and principles is referred to as internalization.
Assimilation	According to Piaget, assimilation is the process of the organism interacting with the environment given the organism's cognitive structure. Assimilation is reuse of schemas to fit new information.
Motives	Needs or desires that energize and direct behavior toward a goal are motives.
Cognition	The intellectual processes through which information is obtained, transformed, stored, retrieved, and otherwise used is cognition.

Go to **Cram101.com** for the Practice Tests for this Chapter.

Affect	A subjective feeling or emotional tone often accompanied by bodily expressions noticeable to others is called affect.
Meta-analysis	In statistics, a meta-analysis combines the results of several studies that address a set of related research hypotheses.
Attribution theory	Attribution theory is concerned with the ways in which people explain the behavior of others. It explores how individuals "attribute" causes to events and how this cognitive perception affects their motivation.
Locus of control	The place to which an individual attributes control over the receiving of reinforcers -either inside or outside the self is referred to as locus of control.
Incentive	An incentive is what is expected once a behavior is performed. An incentive acts as a reinforcer.
Social comparison	Social comparison theory is the idea that individuals learn about and assess themselves by comparison with other people. Research shows that individuals tend to lean more toward social comparisons in situations that are ambiguous.
Insight	Insight refers to a sudden awareness of the relationships among various elements that had previously appeared to be independent of one another.
Csikszentmihalyi	Csikszentmihalyi is noted for his work in the study of happiness, creativity, subjective well-being, and fun, but is best known for his having been the architect of the notion of flow: "... people are most happy when they are in a state of flow--a Zen-like state of total oneness...".
Consciousness	The awareness of the sensations, thoughts, and feelings being experienced at a given moment is called consciousness.
Automaticity	The ability to process information with little or no effort is referred to as automaticity.
Self-awareness	Realization that one's existence and functioning are separate from those of other people and things is called self-awareness.
Anxiety	Anxiety is a complex combination of the feeling of fear, apprehension and worry often accompanied by physical sensations such as palpitations, chest pain and/or shortness of breath.
Ecstasy	Ecstasy as an emotion is to be outside oneself, in a trancelike state in which an individual transcends ordinary consciousness and as a result has a heightened capacity for exceptional thought or experience. Ecstasy also refers to a relatively new hallucinogen that is chemically similar to mescaline and the amphetamines.
Attitude	An enduring mental representation of a person, place, or thing that evokes an emotional response and related behavior is called attitude.
Personality	Personality refers to the pattern of enduring characteristics that differentiates a person, the patterns of behaviors that make each individual unique.
Trait	An enduring personality characteristic that tends to lead to certain behaviors is called a trait. The term trait also means a genetically inherited feature of an organism.
Knowledge base	The general background information a person possesses, which influences most cognitive task performance is called the knowledge base.

Motivation	In psychology, motivation is the driving force (desire) behind all actions of an organism.
Learning	Learning is a relatively permanent change in behavior that results from experience. Thus, to attribute a behavioral change to learning, the change must be relatively permanent and must result from experience.
Locke	In 1690, Locke wrote his Essay Concerning Human Understanding. The essay arugued for empiricism, that ideas come only from experience. In other words, there are no innate ideas. The tabula rasa or blank slate was his metaphor.
Statistics	Statistics is a type of data analysis which practice includes the planning, summarizing, and interpreting of observations of a system possibly followed by predicting or forecasting of future events based on a mathematical model of the system being observed.
Statistic	A statistic is an observable random variable of a sample.
Control group	A group that does not receive the treatment effect in an experiment is referred to as the control group or sometimes as the comparison group.
Anxiety	Anxiety is a complex combination of the feeling of fear, apprehension and worry often accompanied by physical sensations such as palpitations, chest pain and/or shortness of breath.
Questionnaire	A self-report method of data collection or clinical assessment method in which the individual being studied checks off items on a printed list, answers multiple-choice questions, or writes out answers to essay questions aimed at producing a selfdescription is called questionnaire.
Attention	Attention is the cognitive process of selectively concentrating on one thing while ignoring other things. Psychologists have labeled three types of attention: sustained attention, selective attention, and divided attention.
Stroke	A stroke occurs when the blood supply to a part of the brain is suddenly interrupted by occlusion, by hemorrhage, or other causes
Nurture	Nurture refers to the environmental influences on behavior due to nutrition, culture, socioeconomic status, and learning.
Variability	Statistically, variability refers to how much the scores in a distribution spread out, away from the mean.
Social comparison	Social comparison theory is the idea that individuals learn about and assess themselves by comparison with other people. Research shows that individuals tend to lean more toward social comparisons in situations that are ambiguous.
Baseline	Measure of a particular behavior or process taken before the introduction of the independent variable or treatment is called the baseline.
Meta-analysis	In statistics, a meta-analysis combines the results of several studies that address a set of related research hypotheses.
Personality	Personality refers to the pattern of enduring characteristics that differentiates a person, the patterns of behaviors that make each individual unique.
Blocking	If the one of the two members of a compound stimulus fails to produce the CR due to an earlier conditioning of the other member of the compound stimulus, blocking has occurred.
Feedback	Feedback refers to information returned to a person about the effects a response has had.
Distal	Students can set both long-term (distal) and short-term (proximal) goals .
Quantitative	A quantitative property is one that exists in a range of magnitudes, and can therefore be

measured. Measurements of any particular quantitative property are expressed as as a specific quantity, referred to as a unit, multiplied by a number.

Motives	Needs or desires that energize and direct behavior toward a goal are motives.
Motivation	In psychology, motivation is the driving force (desire) behind all actions of an organism.
Intrinsic motivation	Intrinsic motivation causes people to engage in an activity for its own sake. They are subjective factors and include self-determination, curiosity, challenge, effort, and others.
Self-esteem	Self-esteem refers to a person's subjective appraisal of himself or herself as intrinsically positive or negative to some degree.
Society	The social sciences use the term society to mean a group of people that form a semi-closed (or semi-open) social system, in which most interactions are with other individuals belonging to the group.
Moral development	Development regarding rules and conventions about what people should do in their interactions with other people is called moral development.
Representative sample	Representative sample refers to a sample of participants selected from the larger population in such a way that important subgroups within the population are included in the sample in the same proportions as they are found in the larger population.
Cocaine	Cocaine is a crystalline tropane alkaloid that is obtained from the leaves of the coca plant. It is a stimulant of the central nervous system and an appetite suppressant, creating what has been described as a euphoric sense of happiness and increased energy.
Suicide	Suicide behavior is rare in childhood but escalates in adolescence. The suicide rate increases in a linear fashion from adolescence through late adulthood.
Steroid	A steroid is a lipid characterized by a carbon skeleton with four fused rings. Different steroids vary in the functional groups attached to these rings. Hundreds of distinct steroids have been identified in plants and animals. Their most important role in most living systems is as hormones.
Enrichment	Deliberately making an environment more novel, complex, and perceptually or intellectually stimulating is referred to as enrichment.
Learning	Learning is a relatively permanent change in behavior that results from experience. Thus, to attribute a behavioral change to learning, the change must be relatively permanent and must result from experience.
Self-efficacy	Self-efficacy is the belief that one has the capabilities to execute the courses of actions required to manage prospective situations.
Locus of control	The place to which an individual attributes control over the receiving of reinforcers -either inside or outside the self is referred to as locus of control.
Autonomy	Autonomy is the condition of something that does not depend on anything else.
Ego	In Freud's view the Ego serves to balance our primitive needs and our moral beliefs and taboos. Relying on experience, a healthy Ego provides the ability to adapt to reality and interact with the outside world.
Anxiety	Anxiety is a complex combination of the feeling of fear, apprehension and worry often accompanied by physical sensations such as palpitations, chest pain and/or shortness of breath.
Emotion	An emotion is a mental states that arise spontaneously, rather than through conscious effort. They are often accompanied by physiological changes.
Questionnaire	A self-report method of data collection or clinical assessment method in which the individual being studied checks off items on a printed list, answers multiple-choice questions, or writes out answers to essay questions aimed at producing a selfdescription is called

Go to **Cram101.com** for the Practice Tests for this Chapter.

	questionnaire.
Punishment	Punishment is the addtion of a stimulus that reduces the frequency of a response, or the removal of a stimulus that results in a reduction of the response.
Behavioral assessment	Direct measures of an individual's behavior used to describe characteristics indicative of personality are called behavioral assessment.
Positive reinforcement	In positive reinforcement, a stimulus is added and the rate of responding increases.
Reinforcement	In operant conditioning, reinforcement is any change in an environment that (a) occurs after the behavior, (b) seems to make that behavior re-occur more often in the future and (c) that reoccurence of behavior must be the result of the change.
Feedback	Feedback refers to information returned to a person about the effects a response has had.
Correlation	A statistical technique for determining the degree of association between two or more variables is referred to as correlation.
Perception	Perception is the process of acquiring, interpreting, selecting, and organizing sensory information.
Norms	In testing, standards of test performance that permit the comparison of one person's score on the test to the scores of others who have taken the same test are referred to as norms.
Social support	Social Support is the physical and emotional comfort given by family, friends, co-workers and others. Research has identified three main types of social support: emotional, practical, sharing points of view.
Self-worth	In psychology, self-esteem or self-worth refers to a person's subjective appraisal of himself or herself as intrinsically positive or negative to some degree.

Personality	Personality refers to the pattern of enduring characteristics that differentiates a person, the patterns of behaviors that make each individual unique.
Attention	Attention is the cognitive process of selectively concentrating on one thing while ignoring other things. Psychologists have labeled three types of attention: sustained attention, selective attention, and divided attention.
Metabolism	Metabolism is the biochemical modification of chemical compounds in living organisms and cells.
Nervous system	The body's electrochemical communication circuitry, made up of billions of neurons is a nervous system.
Spinal cord	The spinal cord is a part of the vertebrate nervous system that is enclosed in and protected by the vertebral column (it passes through the spinal canal). It consists of nerve cells. The spinal cord carries sensory signals and motor innervation to most of the skeletal muscles in the body.
Brain stem	The brain stem is the stalk of the brain below the cerebral hemispheres. It is the major route for communication between the forebrain and the spinal cord and peripheral nerves. It also controls various functions including respiration, regulation of heart rhythms, and primary aspects of sound localization.
Brain	The brain controls and coordinates most movement, behavior and homeostatic body functions such as heartbeat, blood pressure, fluid balance and body temperature. Functions of the brain are responsible for cognition, emotion, memory, motor learning and other sorts of learning. The brain is primarily made up of two types of cells: glia and neurons.
Peripheral nervous system	The peripheral nervous system consists of the nerves and neurons that serve the limbs and organs. It is not protected by bone or the blood-brain barrier, leaving it exposed to toxins and mechanical injuries. The peripheral nervous system is divided into the somatic nervous system and the autonomic nervous system.
Skeletal muscle	Skeletal muscle is a type of striated muscle, attached to the skeleton. They are used to facilitate movement, by applying force to bones and joints; via contraction. They generally contract voluntarily (via nerve stimulation), although they can contract involuntarily.
Autonomic nervous system	A division of the peripheral nervous system, the autonomic nervous system, regulates glands and activities such as heartbeat, respiration, digestion, and dilation of the pupils. It is responsible for homeostasis, maintaining a relatively constant internal environment .
Gland	A gland is an organ in an animal's body that synthesizes a substance for release such as hormones, often into the bloodstream or into cavities inside the body or its outer surface.
Arousal response	A pattern of measurable physiological changes that helps prepare the body for the possible expenditure of a large amount of energy is referred to as the arousal response.
Central nervous system	The vertebrate central nervous system consists of the brain and spinal cord.
Ascending reticular activating system	Ascending reticular activating system are the afferent fibers running through the reticular formation that influence physiological arousal.
Reticular activating system	The reticular activating system is the part of the brain believed to be the center of arousal and motivation. It is situated between the brain stem and the central nervous system (CNS).
Cerebral cortex	The cerebral cortex is the outermost layer of the cerebrum and has a grey color. It is made

Go to **Cram101.com** for the Practice Tests for this Chapter.

up of four lobes and it is involved in many complex brain functions including memory, perceptual awareness, "thinking", language and consciousness. The cerebral cortex receives sensory information from many different sensory organs eg: eyes, ears, etc. and processes the information.

Hypothalamus	The hypothalamus is a region of the brain located below the thalamus, forming the major portion of the ventral region of the diencephalon and functioning to regulate certain metabolic processes and other autonomic activities.
Neuron	The neuron is the primary cell of the nervous system. They are found in the brain, the spinal cord, in the nerves and ganglia of the peripheral nervous system. It is a specialized cell that conducts impulses through the nervous system and contains three major parts: cell body, dendrites, and an axon. It can have many dendrites but only one axon.
Occipital lobe	The occipital lobe is the smallest of four true lobes in the human brain. Located in the rearmost portion of the skull, the occipital lobe is part of the forebrain structure. It is the visual processing center.
Temporal lobe	The temporal lobe is part of the cerebrum. It lies at the side of the brain, beneath the lateral or Sylvian fissure. Adjacent areas in the superior, posterior and lateral parts of the temporal lobe are involved in high-level auditory processing.
Parietal lobe	The parietal lobe is positioned above (superior to) the occipital lobe and behind (posterior to) the frontal lobe. It plays important roles in integrating sensory information from various senses, and in the manipulation of objects.
Frontal lobe	The frontal lobe comprises four major folds of cortical tissue: the precentral gyrus, superior gyrus and the middle gyrus of the frontal gyri, the inferior frontal gyrus. It has been found to play a part in impulse control, judgement, language, memory, motor function, problem solving, sexual behavior, socialization and spontaneity.
Lobes	The four major sections of the cerebral cortex: frontal, parietal, temporal, and occipital are called lobes.
Emotion	An emotion is a mental states that arise spontaneously, rather than through conscious effort. They are often accompanied by physiological changes.
Electroencep-alogram	Electroencephalography is the neurophysiologic measurement of the electrical activity of the brain by recording from electrodes placed on the scalp, or in the special cases on the cortex. The resulting traces are known as an electroencephalogram and represent so-called brainwaves.
Amplitude	Amplitude is a nonnegative scalar measure of a wave's magnitude of oscillation.
Midbrain	Located between the hindbrain and forebrain, a region in which many nerve-fiber systems ascend and descend to connect the higher and lower portions of the brain is referred to as midbrain. It is archipallian in origin, meaning its general architecture is shared with the most ancient of vertebrates. Dopamine produced in the subtantia nigra plays a role in motivation and habituation of species from humans to the most elementary animals such as insects.
Reticular formation	Reticular formation is a part of the brain which is involved in stereotypical actions, such as walking, sleeping, and lying down. The reticular formation, phylogenetically one of the oldest portions of the brain, is a poorly-differentiated area of the brain stem.
Sensorimotor	The first of Piaget's stages is the Sensorimotor stage. This stage typically ranges from birth to 2 years. In this stage, children experience the world through their senses. During this stage, object permanence and stranger anxiety develop.
Biological	Biological psychology works on the basis that there is an organic basis to mental processes,

Go to **Cram101.com** for the Practice Tests for this Chapter.

psychology	and that this requires an understanding of the way that mental processes are instantiated in the brain.
Axon	An axon, or "nerve fiber," is a long slender projection of a nerve cell, or "neuron," which conducts electrical impulses away from the neuron's cell body or soma.
Polygraph	A polygraph is a device which measures and records several physiological variables such as blood pressure, heart rate, respiration and skin conductivity while a series of questions is being asked, in an attempt to detect lies.
Parasympathetic	The parasympathetic nervous system is one of two divisions of the autonomic nervous system. It conserves energy as it slows the heart rate, increases intestinal and gland activity, and relaxes sphincter muscles. In another words, it acts to reverse the effects of the Sympathetic nervous system.
Sympathetic	The sympathetic nervous system activates what is often termed the "fight or flight response". It is an automatic regulation system, that is, one that operates without the intervention of conscious thought.
Norepinephrine	Norepinephrine is released from the adrenal glands as a hormone into the blood, but it is also a neurotransmitter in the nervous system. As a stress hormone, it affects parts of the human brain where attention and impulsivity are controlled. Along with epinephrine, this compound effects the fight-or-flight response, activating the sympathetic nervous system to directly increase heart rate, release energy from fat, and increase muscle readiness.
Acetylcholine	The chemical compound acetylcholine was the first neurotransmitter to be identified. It plays a role in learning, memory, and rapid eye movement sleep and causes the skeletal muscle fibers to contract.
Nerve	A nerve is an enclosed, cable-like bundle of nerve fibers or axons, which includes the glia that ensheath the axons in myelin. Neurons are sometimes called nerve cells, though this term is technically imprecise since many neurons do not form nerves.
Hormone	A hormone is a chemical messenger from one cell (or group of cells) to another. The best known are those produced by endocrine glands, but they are produced by nearly every organ system. The function of hormones is to serve as a signal to the target cells; the action of the hormone is determined by the pattern of secretion and the signal transduction of the receiving tissue.
Anxiety	Anxiety is a complex combination of the feeling of fear, apprehension and worry often accompanied by physical sensations such as palpitations, chest pain and/or shortness of breath.
Alarm reaction	The first stage of the general adaptation syndrome, which is triggered by the impact of a stressor and characterized by sympathetic activity is called the alarm reaction.
Epinephrine	Epinephrine is a hormone and a neurotransmitter. Epinephrine plays a central role in the short-term stress reaction—the physiological response to threatening or exciting conditions. It is secreted by the adrenal medulla. When released into the bloodstream, epinephrine binds to multiple receptors and has numerous effects throughout the body.
Cognition	The intellectual processes through which information is obtained, transformed, stored, retrieved, and otherwise used is cognition.
Affect	A subjective feeling or emotional tone often accompanied by bodily expressions noticeable to others is called affect.
Homeostasis	Homeostasis is the property of an open system, especially living organisms, to regulate its internal environment so as to maintain a stable condition, by means of multiple dynamic equilibrium adjustments controlled by interrelated regulation mechanisms.

Deep sleep	Deep sleep refers to stage 4 sleep; the deepest form of normal sleep.
Theta wave	A theta wave is an electroencephalogram pattern normally produced while awake but relaxed or drowsy. The pattern has a frequency of 3.5 to 7.5 Hz. They are strong during internal focus, meditation, prayer, and spiritual awareness.
Delta wave	A delta wave is a large, slow brain wave associated with deep sleep. They are present only in stage-three sleep, stage -four sleep, and coma.
Alpha wave	The brain wave associated with deep relaxation is referred to as the alpha wave. Recorded by electroencephalography (EEG) , they are synchronous and coherent (regular like sawtooth) and in the frequency range of 8 - 12 Hz. It is also called Berger's wave in memory of the founder of EEG.
Beta wave	A low amplitude brain beta wave with multiple and varying frequencies is often associated with active, busy or anxious thinking and active concentration.
Correlation	A statistical technique for determining the degree of association between two or more variables is referred to as correlation.
Electromyograph	Electromyography (EMG) is a medical technique for measuring muscle response to nervous stimulation. EMG is performed using an instrument called an electromyograph, to produce a record called an electromyogram. An electromyograph detects the electrical potential generated by muscle cells when these cells contract.
Electromyography	Electromyography is a medical technique for measuring muscle response to nervous stimulation.
Galvanic skin response	Galvanic skin response is a method of measuring the electrical resistance of the skin and interpreting it as an image of activity in certain parts of the body.
Electrode	Any device used to electrically stimulate nerve tissue or to record its activity is an electrode.
Stimulus	A change in an environmental condition that elicits a response is a stimulus.

Go to **Cram101.com** for the Practice Tests for this Chapter.
And, **NEVER** highlight a book again!

Attention	Attention is the cognitive process of selectively concentrating on one thing while ignoring other things. Psychologists have labeled three types of attention: sustained attention, selective attention, and divided attention.
Personality	Personality refers to the pattern of enduring characteristics that differentiates a person, the patterns of behaviors that make each individual unique.
Stroke	A stroke occurs when the blood supply to a part of the brain is suddenly interrupted by occlusion, by hemorrhage, or other causes
Information processing	Information processing is an approach to the goal of understanding human thinking. The essence of the approach is to see cognition as being essentially computational in nature, with mind being the software and the brain being the hardware.
Stimulus	A change in an environmental condition that elicits a response is a stimulus.
Brain	The brain controls and coordinates most movement, behavior and homeostatic body functions such as heartbeat, blood pressure, fluid balance and body temperature. Functions of the brain are responsible for cognition, emotion, memory, motor learning and other sorts of learning. The brain is primarily made up of two types of cells: glia and neurons.
Information processing model	The essence of the information processing model is to see cognition as being essentially computational in nature, with mind being the software and the brain being the hardware.
Retrieval	Retrieval is the location of stored information and its subsequent return to consciousness. It is the third stage of information processing.
Sensory register	Sensory register involves two components: iconic memory: the storage of visual information, lasting about half a second; and, echoic memory: the storage of auditory information, lasting up to two seconds. Information from the environment is filtered through this sensory register and passed on to the short-term memory circuit.
Short-term memory	Short-term memory is that part of memory which stores a limited amount of information for a limited amount of time (roughly 30-45 seconds). The second key concept associated with a short-term memory is that it has a finite capacity.
Permanent memory	Hebb did not believe that any chemical process could occur fast enough to accomodate immediate memory yet remain stable enough to accomodate permanent memory. Thus the notion of two memory systems was proposed: long-term memory (LTM), and short-term memory (STM).
Long-term memory	Long-term memory is memory that lasts from over 30 seconds to years.
Working Memory	Working memory is the collection of structures and processes in the brain used for temporarily storing and manipulating information. Working memory consists of both memory for items that are currently being processed, and components governing attention and directing the processing itself.
Chunking	In cognitive psychology and mnemonics, chunking refers to a strategy for making more efficient use of short-term memory by recoding information.
Pitch	Pitch is the psychological interpretation of a sound or musical tone corresponding to its physical frequency
Selective attention	Selective attention is a type of attention which involves focusing on a specific aspect of a scene while ignoring other aspects.
Mental disorder	Mental disorder refers to a disturbance in a person's emotions, drives, thought processes, or behavior that involves serious and relatively prolonged distress and/or impairment in ability to function, is not simply a normal response to some event or set of events in the person's environment.

Go to **Cram101.com** for the Practice Tests for this Chapter.

Norepinephrine	Norepinephrine is released from the adrenal glands as a hormone into the blood, but it is also a neurotransmitter in the nervous system. As a stress hormone, it affects parts of the human brain where attention and impulsivity are controlled. Along with epinephrine, this compound effects the fight-or-flight response, activating the sympathetic nervous system to directly increase heart rate, release energy from fat, and increase muscle readiness.
Schizophrenia	Schizophrenia is characterized by persistent defects in the perception or expression of reality. A person suffering from untreated schizophrenia typically demonstrates grossly disorganized thinking, and may also experience delusions or auditory hallucinations
Depression	In everyday language depression refers to any downturn in mood, which may be relatively transitory and perhaps due to something trivial. This is differentiated from Clinical depression which is marked by symptoms that last two weeks or more and are so severe that they interfere with daily living.
Dopamine	Dopamine is critical to the way the brain controls our movements and is a crucial part of the basal ganglia motor loop. It is commonly associated with the 'pleasure system' of the brain, providing feelings of enjoyment and reinforcement to motivate us to do, or continue doing, certain activities.
Blocking	If the one of the two members of a compound stimulus fails to produce the CR due to an earlier conditioning of the other member of the compound stimulus, blocking has occurred.
Reaction time	The amount of time required to respond to a stimulus is referred to as reaction time.
Learning	Learning is a relatively permanent change in behavior that results from experience. Thus, to attribute a behavioral change to learning, the change must be relatively permanent and must result from experience.
Individual differences	Individual differences psychology studies the ways in which individual people differ in their behavior. This is distinguished from other aspects of psychology in that although psychology is ostensibly a study of individuals, modern psychologists invariably study groups.
Peripheral vision	Peripheral vision is that part of vision that occurs outside the very center of gaze. Peripheral vision is weak in humans, especially at distinguishing color and shape. This is because the density of receptor cells on the retina is greatest at the center and lowest at the edges
Correlation	A statistical technique for determining the degree of association between two or more variables is referred to as correlation.
Anxiety	Anxiety is a complex combination of the feeling of fear, apprehension and worry often accompanied by physical sensations such as palpitations, chest pain and/or shortness of breath.
Csikszentmihalyi	Csikszentmihalyi is noted for his work in the study of happiness, creativity, subjective well-being, and fun, but is best known for his having been the architect of the notion of flow: "... people are most happy when they are in a state of flow--a Zen-like state of total oneness...".
Behavioral assessment	Direct measures of an individual's behavior used to describe characteristics indicative of personality are called behavioral assessment.
Self-report method	The self-report method is an experimental design in which the people being studied are asked to rate or describe their own behaviors or mental states.
Personality trait	According to the Diagnostic and Statistical Manual of the American Psychiatric Association, a personality trait is a "prominent aspect of personality that is exhibited in a wide range of important social and personal contexts. ...".

Trait	An enduring personality characteristic that tends to lead to certain behaviors is called a trait. The term trait also means a genetically inherited feature of an organism.
Attentional processes	In Bandura's theory of vicarious learning, any activity by an observer that aids in the observation of relevant aspects of a model's behavior and its consequences is referred to as attentional processes.
Validity	The extent to which a test measures what it is intended to measure is called validity.
Dewey	Dewey is one of the three central figures in American pragmatism though he did not identify himself as a pragmatist per se, and instead referred to his philosophy as "instrumentalism". He established the first major educational psychology laboratory in the United States, at the University of Chicago in 1894.
Thought stopping	Thought stopping is a behavioral approach that uses aversive stimuli to interrupt or prevent upsetting thoughts.
Attitude	An enduring mental representation of a person, place, or thing that evokes an emotional response and related behavior is called attitude.
Consciousness	The awareness of the sensations, thoughts, and feelings being experienced at a given moment is called consciousness.
Hypothesis	A specific statement about behavior or mental processes that is testable through research is a hypothesis.
Dissociative disorder	Psychological dysfunctions characterized by the separation of critical personality facets that are normally integrated, allowing stress avoidance by escape is a dissociative disorder.
Clinical psychology	Clinical psychology is involved in the diagnosis, assessment, and treatment of patients with mental or behavioral disorders, and conducts research in these various areas.
Dissociation	Dissociation is a psychological state or condition in which certain thoughts, emotions, sensations, or memories are separated from the rest.
Structured interview	Structured interview refers to an interview in which the questions are set out in a prescribed fashion for the interviewer. It assists professionals in making diagnostic decisions based upon standardized criteria.
Feedback	Feedback refers to information returned to a person about the effects a response has had.
Variable	A variable refers to a measurable factor, characteristic, or attribute of an individual or a system.
Stages	Stages represent relatively discrete periods of time in which functioning is qualitatively different from functioning at other periods.

Personality	Personality refers to the pattern of enduring characteristics that differentiates a person, the patterns of behaviors that make each individual unique.
Psychological testing	Psychological testing is a field characterized by the use of small samples of behavior in order to infer larger generalizations about a given individual. The technical term for psychological testing is psychometrics.
Correlation	A statistical technique for determining the degree of association between two or more variables is referred to as correlation.
Neo-Freudian	The Neo-Freudian psychologists were those followers of Sigmund Freud who accepted the basic tenets of his theory of psychoanalysis but altered it in some way.
Jung	Jung was in some aspects a response to Sigmund Freud's psychoanalysis. He proposed and developed the concepts of the extroverted and introverted personality, archetypes, and the collective unconscious. His work has been influential in psychiatry and in the study of religion, literature, and related fields.
Psychotherapy	Psychotherapy is a set of techniques based on psychological principles intended to improve mental health, emotional or behavioral issues.
Psychodynamic	Most psychodynamic approaches are centered around the idea of a maladapted function developed early in life (usually childhood) which are at least in part unconscious. This maladapted function (a.k.a. defense mechanism) does not do well in place of a normal/healthy one.
Motives	Needs or desires that energize and direct behavior toward a goal are motives.
Superego	Frued's third psychic structure, which functions as a moral guardian and sets forth high standards for behavior is the superego.
Ego	In Freud's view the Ego serves to balance our primitive needs and our moral beliefs and taboos. Relying on experience, a healthy Ego provides the ability to adapt to reality and interact with the outside world.
Socialization	Social rules and social relations are created, communicated, and changed in verbal and nonverbal ways creating social complexity useful in identifying outsiders and intelligent breeding partners. The process of learning these skills is called socialization.
Society	The social sciences use the term society to mean a group of people that form a semi-closed (or semi-open) social system, in which most interactions are with other individuals belonging to the group.
Instinct	Instinct is the word used to describe inherent dispositions towards particular actions. They are generally an inherited pattern of responses or reactions to certain kinds of situations.
Instinct theory	The notion that human behavior is motivated by certain innate tendencies, or instincts, shared by all individuals is an instinct theory.
Social learning theory	Social learning theory explains the process of gender typing in terms of observation, imitation, and role playing .
Psychoanalytic theory	Psychoanalytic theory is a general term for approaches to psychoanalysis which attempt to provide a conceptual framework more-or-less independent of clinical practice rather than based on empirical analysis of clinical cases.
Social learning	Social learning is learning that occurs as a function of observing, retaining and replicating behavior observed in others. Although social learning can occur at any stage in life, it is thought to be particularly important during childhood, particularly as authority becomes important.
Psychoanalytic	Freud's theory that unconscious forces act as determinants of personality is called

	psychoanalytic theory. The theory is a developmental theory characterized by critical stages of development.
Predisposition	Predisposition refers to an inclination or diathesis to respond in a certain way, either inborn or acquired. In abnormal psychology, it is a factor that lowers the ability to withstand stress and inclines the individual toward pathology.
Learning	Learning is a relatively permanent change in behavior that results from experience. Thus, to attribute a behavioral change to learning, the change must be relatively permanent and must result from experience.
Personality trait	According to the Diagnostic and Statistical Manual of the American Psychiatric Association, a personality trait is a "prominent aspect of personality that is exhibited in a wide range of important social and personal contexts. ...".
Trait	An enduring personality characteristic that tends to lead to certain behaviors is called a trait. The term trait also means a genetically inherited feature of an organism.
Behaviorism	The school of psychology that defines psychology as the study of observable behavior and studies relationships between stimuli and responses is called behaviorism. Behaviorism relied heavily on animal research and stated the same principles governed the behavior of both nonhumans and humans.
Skinner	Skinner conducted research on shaping behavior through positive and negative reinforcement, and demonstrated operant conditioning, a technique which he developed in contrast with classical conditioning.
Hull	Hull is best known for the Drive Reduction Theory which postulated that behavior occurs in response to primary drives such as hunger, thirst, sexual interest, etc. When the goal of the drive is attained the drive is reduced. This reduction of drive serves as a reinforcer for learning.
Stimulus	A change in an environmental condition that elicits a response is a stimulus.
Social reinforcement	Praise, attention, approval, and/or affection from others is referred to as social reinforcement.
Reinforcement	In operant conditioning, reinforcement is any change in an environment that (a) occurs after the behavior, (b) seems to make that behavior re-occur more often in the future and (c) that reoccurence of behavior must be the result of the change.
Modeling	A type of behavior learned through observation of others demonstrating the same behavior is modeling.
Bandura	Bandura is best known for his work on social learning theory or Social Cognitivism. His famous Bobo doll experiment illustrated that people learn from observing others.
Observational learning	The acquisition of knowledge and skills through the observation of others rather than by means of direct experience is observational learning. Four major processes are thought to influence the observational learning: attentional, retentional, behavioral production, and motivational.
Attention	Attention is the cognitive process of selectively concentrating on one thing while ignoring other things. Psychologists have labeled three types of attention: sustained attention, selective attention, and divided attention.
Carl Rogers	Carl Rogers was instrumental in the development of non-directive psychotherapy, also known as "client-centered" psychotherapy. Rogers' basic tenets were unconditional positive regard, genuineness, and empathic understanding, with each demonstrated by the counselor.
Humanistic	Humanistic refers to any system of thought focused on subjective experience and human

problems and potentials.

Maslow	Maslow is mostly noted today for his proposal of a hierarchy of human needs which he often presented as a pyramid. Maslow was an instrumental player in the formation of the humanistic movement, also known as the third force in psychology.
Human nature	Human nature is the fundamental nature and substance of humans, as well as the range of human behavior that is believed to be invariant over long periods of time and across very different cultural contexts.
Self-actualization	Self-actualization (a term originated by Kurt Goldstein) is the instinctual need of a human to make the most of their unique abilities. Maslow described it as follows: Self Actualization is the intrinsic growth of what is already in the organism, or more accurately, of what the organism is.
Innate	Innate behavior is not learned or influenced by the environment, rather, it is present or predisposed at birth.
Openness to Experience	Openness to Experience, one of the big-five traits, describes a dimension of cognitive style that distinguishes imaginative, creative people from down-to-earth, conventional people.
Perception	Perception is the process of acquiring, interpreting, selecting, and organizing sensory information.
Self-concept	Self-concept refers to domain-specific evaluations of the self where a domain may be academics, athletics, etc.
Raymond Cattell	Raymond Cattell proposed that 16 factors underlie human personality. He called these 16 factors source traits because he believed that they provide the underlying source for the surface behaviors that we think of as personality.
Hans Eysenck	Hans Eysenck using Factor Analysis concluded that all human traits can be broken down into two distinct categories: 1. Extroversion-Introversion, 2. Neuroticism. He called these categories Supertraits.
Allport	Allport was a trait theorist. Those traits he believed to predominate a person's personality were called central traits. Traits such that one could be indentifed by the trait, were referred to as cardinal traits. Central traits and cardinal traits are influenced by environmental factors.
Extraversion	Extraversion, one of the big-five personailty traits, is marked by pronounced engagement with the external world. They are people who enjoy being with people, are full of energy, and often experience positive emotions.
Neuroticism	Eysenck's use of the term neuroticism (or Emotional Stability) was proposed as the dimension describing individual differences in the predisposition towards neurotic disorder.
Questionnaire	A self-report method of data collection or clinical assessment method in which the individual being studied checks off items on a printed list, answers multiple-choice questions, or writes out answers to essay questions aimed at producing a selfdescription is called questionnaire.
Inference	Inference is the act or process of drawing a conclusion based solely on what one already knows.
Thematic Apperception Test	The Thematic Apperception Test uses a standard series of provocative yet ambiguous pictures about which the subject must tell a story. Each story is carefully analyzed to uncover underlying needs, attitudes, and patterns of reaction.
Apperception	A newly experienced sensation is related to past experiences to form an understood situation. For Wundt, consciousness is composed of two "stages:" There is a large capacity working

Go to **Cram101.com** for the Practice Tests for this Chapter.

101

	memory called the Blickfeld and the narrower consciousness called Apperception, or selective attention.
Rorschach	The Rorschach inkblot test is a method of psychological evaluation. It is a projective test associated with the Freudian school of thought. Psychologists use this test to try to probe the unconscious minds of their patients.
Projective test	A projective test is a personality test designed to let a person respond to ambiguous stimuli, presumably revealing hidden emotions and internal conflicts. This is different from an "objective test" in which responses are analyzed according to a universal standard rather than an individual psychiatrist's judgement.
Psychiatrist	A psychiatrist is a physician who specializes in the diagnosis and treatment of psychological disorders.
Personality disorder	A mental disorder characterized by a set of inflexible, maladaptive personality traits that keep a person from functioning properly in society is referred to as a personality disorder.
Population	Population refers to all members of a well-defined group of organisms, events, or things.
Minnesota Multiphasic Personality Inventory	The Minnesota Multiphasic Personality Inventory is the most frequently used test in the mental health fields. This assessment or test helps identify personal, social, and behavioral problems in psychiatric patients. This test helps provide relevant information to aid in problem identification, diagnosis, and treatment planning for the patient.
Personality inventory	A self-report questionnaire by which an examinee indicates whether statements assessing habitual tendencies apply to him or her is referred to as a personality inventory.
Depression	In everyday language depression refers to any downturn in mood, which may be relatively transitory and perhaps due to something trivial. This is differentiated from Clinical depression which is marked by symptoms that last two weeks or more and are so severe that they interfere with daily living.
Factor analysis	Factor analysis is a statistical technique that originated in psychometrics. The objective is to explain the most of the variability among a number of observable random variables in terms of a smaller number of unobservable random variables called factors.
Big five	The big five factors of personality are Openness to experience, Conscientiousness, Extraversion, Agreeableness, and Emotional Stability.
Conscientiou- ness	Conscientiousness is one of the dimensions of the five-factor model of personality and individual differences involving being organized, thorough, and reliable as opposed to careless, negligent, and unreliable.
Agreeableness	Agreeableness, one of the big-five personality traits, reflects individual differences in concern with cooperation and social harmony. It is the degree individuals value getting along with others.
Standardized score	A score that is expressed in terms of the number of standard deviations the original score is from the mean of the original scores is a standardized score.
Raw score	A raw score is an original datum that has not been transformed – for example, the original result obtained by a student on a test (i.e., the number of correctly answered items) as opposed to that score after transformation to a standard score or percentile rank or the like.
Reliability	Reliability means the extent to which a test produces a consistent , reproducible score .
Validity	The extent to which a test measures what it is intended to measure is called validity.
Variable	A variable refers to a measurable factor, characteristic, or attribute of an individual or a

system.

Variance	The degree to which scores differ among individuals in a distribution of scores is the variance.
Psychometric	Psychometric study is concerned with the theory and technique of psychological measurement, which includes the measurement of knowledge, abilities, attitudes, and personality traits. The field is primarily concerned with the study of differences between individuals
Statistics	Statistics is a type of data analysis which practice includes the planning, summarizing, and interpreting of observations of a system possibly followed by predicting or forecasting of future events based on a mathematical model of the system being observed.
Statistic	A statistic is an observable random variable of a sample.
Hypothesis	A specific statement about behavior or mental processes that is testable through research is a hypothesis.
Anxiety	Anxiety is a complex combination of the feeling of fear, apprehension and worry often accompanied by physical sensations such as palpitations, chest pain and/or shortness of breath.
Natural selection	Natural selection is a process by which biological populations are altered over time, as a result of the propagation of heritable traits that affect the capacity of individual organisms to survive and reproduce.
Self-worth	In psychology, self-esteem or self-worth refers to a person's subjective appraisal of himself or herself as intrinsically positive or negative to some degree.
Harlow	Harlow and his famous wire and cloth surrogate mother monkey studies demonstrated that the need for affection created a stronger bond between mother and infant than did physical needs. He also found that the more discrimination problems the monkeys solved, the better they became at solving them.
Stereotype	A stereotype is considered to be a group concept, held by one social group about another. They are often used in a negative or prejudicial sense and are frequently used to justify certain discriminatory behaviors. This allows powerful social groups to legitimize and protect their dominant position
Autonomy	Autonomy is the condition of something that does not depend on anything else.
Personality type	A persistent style of complex behaviors defined by a group of related traits is referred to as a personality type. Myer Friedman and his co-workers first defined personality types in the 1950s. Friedman classified people into 2 categories, Type A and Type B.
Personality test	A personality test aims to describe aspects of a person's character that remain stable across situations.
Reasoning	Reasoning is the act of using reason to derive a conclusion from certain premises. There are two main methods to reach a conclusion, deductive reasoning and inductive reasoning.
Heterogeneous	A heterogeneous compound, mixture, or other such object is one that consists of many different items, which are often not easily sorted or separated, though they are clearly distinct.
Homogeneous	In biology homogeneous has a meaning similar to its meaning in mathematics. Generally it means "the same" or "of the same quality or general property".
Generalization	In conditioning, the tendency for a conditioned response to be evoked by stimuli that are similar to the stimulus to which the response was conditioned is a generalization. The greater the similarity among the stimuli, the greater the probability of generalization.

Go to **Cram101.com** for the Practice Tests for this Chapter.

Normative	The term normative is used to describe the effects of those structures of culture which regulate the function of social activity.
Theories	Theories are logically self-consistent models or frameworks describing the behavior of a certain natural or social phenomenon. They are broad explanations and predictions concerning phenomena of interest.
Motivation	In psychology, motivation is the driving force (desire) behind all actions of an organism.
Basic research	Basic research has as its primary objective the advancement of knowledge and the theoretical understanding of the relations among variables . It is exploratory and often driven by the researcher's curiosity, interest or hunch.
Source traits	Cattell's name for the traits that make up the most basic personality structure and causes of behavior is source traits.
Dependent variable	A measure of an assumed effect of an independent variable is called the dependent variable.
Psychological test	Psychological test refers to a standardized measure of a sample of a person's behavior.

56

Go to **Cram101.com** for the Practice Tests for this Chapter.

Personality	Personality refers to the pattern of enduring characteristics that differentiates a person, the patterns of behaviors that make each individual unique.
Personality trait	According to the Diagnostic and Statistical Manual of the American Psychiatric Association, a personality trait is a "prominent aspect of personality that is exhibited in a wide range of important social and personal contexts. ...".
Trait	An enduring personality characteristic that tends to lead to certain behaviors is called a trait. The term trait also means a genetically inherited feature of an organism.
Anxiety	Anxiety is a complex combination of the feeling of fear, apprehension and worry often accompanied by physical sensations such as palpitations, chest pain and/or shortness of breath.
Meta-analysis	In statistics, a meta-analysis combines the results of several studies that address a set of related research hypotheses.
Effect size	An effect size is the strength or magnitude of the difference between two sets of data or, in outcome studies, between two time points for the same population. (The degree to which the null hypothesis is false).
Variable	A variable refers to a measurable factor, characteristic, or attribute of an individual or a system.
Attention	Attention is the cognitive process of selectively concentrating on one thing while ignoring other things. Psychologists have labeled three types of attention: sustained attention, selective attention, and divided attention.
Personality inventory	A self-report questionnaire by which an examinee indicates whether statements assessing habitual tendencies apply to him or her is referred to as a personality inventory.
Depression	In everyday language depression refers to any downturn in mood, which may be relatively transitory and perhaps due to something trivial. This is differentiated from Clinical depression which is marked by symptoms that last two weeks or more and are so severe that they interfere with daily living.
Affect	A subjective feeling or emotional tone often accompanied by bodily expressions noticeable to others is called affect.
Normative	The term normative is used to describe the effects of those structures of culture which regulate the function of social activity.
Population	Population refers to all members of a well-defined group of organisms, events, or things.
Self-esteem	Self-esteem refers to a person's subjective appraisal of himself or herself as intrinsically positive or negative to some degree.
Motivation	In psychology, motivation is the driving force (desire) behind all actions of an organism.
Standard deviation	In probability and statistics, the standard deviation is the most commonly used measure of statistical dispersion. Simply put, it measures how spread out the values in a data set are.
Stimulus	A change in an environmental condition that elicits a response is a stimulus.

Signal detection theory	Signal detection theory is a means to quantify the ability to discern between signal and noise. According to the theory, there are a number of psychological determiners of how we will detect a signal, and where our threshold levels will be. Experience, expectations, physiological state (e.g, fatigue) and other factors affect thresholds.
Primary appraisal	A primary appraisal is an evaluation of the significance of a potentially stressful event according to how it will affect one's well-being-whether it is perceived as irrelevant or as involving harm or loss, threat, or challenge.
Drive Theory	Drive Theory states that due to the unpredictable nature of people, a person performing a task rarely knows for certain what others are going to do in response. This creates a state of arousal that in some cases will facilitate performance, while in other cases it will inhibit performance.
Eustress	Selye called negative stress distress and positive stress eustress.
Anxiety	Anxiety is a complex combination of the feeling of fear, apprehension and worry often accompanied by physical sensations such as palpitations, chest pain and/or shortness of breath.
Emotion	An emotion is a mental states that arise spontaneously, rather than through conscious effort. They are often accompanied by physiological changes.
Affect	A subjective feeling or emotional tone often accompanied by bodily expressions noticeable to others is called affect.
Trait	An enduring personality characteristic that tends to lead to certain behaviors is called a trait. The term trait also means a genetically inherited feature of an organism.
Mesomorphic	The mesomorphic body type is centered around muscle and the circulatory system and has well developed muscles. The mesomorphic person has a somatotonic temperament, and is courageous, energetic, active, dynamic, assertive, aggressive, competitive, and often a risk taker.
Basic anxiety	Basic anxiety is a child's insecurity and doubt when a parent is indifferent, unloving, or disparaging. This anxiety, according to Horney, leads the child to a basic hostility toward his or her parents. The child may then become neurotic as an adult.
Learning	Learning is a relatively permanent change in behavior that results from experience. Thus, to attribute a behavioral change to learning, the change must be relatively permanent and must result from experience.
Selye	Selye did much important theoretical work on the non-specific response of the organism to stress. Selye discovered and documented that stress differs from other physical responses in that stress is stressful whether the one receives good or bad news, whether the impulse is positive or negative. He called negative stress distress and positive stress eustress.
Stimulus	A change in an environmental condition that elicits a response is a stimulus.
Cognition	The intellectual processes through which information is obtained, transformed, stored, retrieved, and otherwise used is cognition.
Perception	Perception is the process of acquiring, interpreting, selecting, and organizing sensory information.
Fisher	Fisher was a eugenicist, evolutionary biologist, geneticist and statistician. He has been described as "The greatest of Darwin's successors", and a genius who almost single-handedly created the foundations for modern statistical science inventing the techniques of maximum likelihood and analysis of variance.
Personality	Personality refers to the pattern of enduring characteristics that differentiates a person, the patterns of behaviors that make each individual unique.

Self-esteem	Self-esteem refers to a person's subjective appraisal of himself or herself as intrinsically positive or negative to some degree.
Antecedents	In behavior modification, events that typically precede the target response are called antecedents.
Variable	A variable refers to a measurable factor, characteristic, or attribute of an individual or a system.
Ego	In Freud's view the Ego serves to balance our primitive needs and our moral beliefs and taboos. Relying on experience, a healthy Ego provides the ability to adapt to reality and interact with the outside world.
Direct observation	Direct observation refers to assessing behavior through direct surveillance.
Construct	A generalized concept, such as anxiety or gravity, is a construct.
Behavioral assessment	Direct measures of an individual's behavior used to describe characteristics indicative of personality are called behavioral assessment.
Psychophysiology	Psychophysiology is the science of understanding the link between psychology and physiology. Psychophysiology is different from physiological psychology in that psychophysiology looks at the way psychological activities produce physiological responses, while physiological psychology looks at the physiological mechanisms which lead to psychological activity.
Attention	Attention is the cognitive process of selectively concentrating on one thing while ignoring other things. Psychologists have labeled three types of attention: sustained attention, selective attention, and divided attention.
Correlation	A statistical technique for determining the degree of association between two or more variables is referred to as correlation.
Nervous system	The body's electrochemical communication circuitry, made up of billions of neurons is a nervous system.
Sympathetic	The sympathetic nervous system activates what is often termed the "fight or flight response". It is an automatic regulation system, that is, one that operates without the intervention of conscious thought.
Yerkes	Yerkes worked in the field of comparative psychology. He is best known for studying the intelligence and social behavior of gorillas and chimpanzees. Joining with John D. Dodson, he developed the Yerkes-Dodson law relating arousal to performance.
Discrimination	In Learning theory, discrimination refers the ability to distinguish between a conditioned stimulus and other stimuli. It can be brought about by extensive training or differential reinforcement. In social terms, it is the denial of privileges to a person or a group on the basis of prejudice.
Brightness	The dimension of visual sensation that is dependent on the intensity of light reflected from a surface and that corresponds to the amplitude of the light wave is called brightness.
Yerkes-Dodson	The Yerkes-Dodson law shows an empirical relationship between arousal and performance. Performance increases with cognitive arousal but only to a certain point: when levels of arousal become too high, performance will decrease. A corollary is that there is an optimal level of arousal for a given task.
Reaction time	The amount of time required to respond to a stimulus is referred to as reaction time.
Pitch	Pitch is the psychological interpretation of a sound or musical tone corresponding to its physical frequency

Go to **Cram101.com** for the Practice Tests for this Chapter.

Theories	Theories are logically self-consistent models or frameworks describing the behavior of a certain natural or social phenomenon. They are broad explanations and predictions concerning phenomena of interest.
Brain	The brain controls and coordinates most movement, behavior and homeostatic body functions such as heartbeat, blood pressure, fluid balance and body temperature. Functions of the brain are responsible for cognition, emotion, memory, motor learning and other sorts of learning. The brain is primarily made up of two types of cells: glia and neurons.
Information processing	Information processing is an approach to the goal of understanding human thinking. The essence of the approach is to see cognition as being essentially computational in nature, with mind being the software and the brain being the hardware.
Channel capacity	Channel capacity, is the amount of discrete information bits that can be reliably transmitted over a channel.
Maladaptive	In psychology, a behavior or trait is adaptive when it helps an individual adjust and function well within their social environment. A maladaptive behavior or trait is counterproductive to the individual.
Affective	Affective is the way people react emotionally, their ability to feel another living thing's pain or joy.
Predisposition	Predisposition refers to an inclination or diathesis to respond in a certain way, either inborn or acquired. In abnormal psychology, it is a factor that lowers the ability to withstand stress and inclines the individual toward pathology.

Anxiety	Anxiety is a complex combination of the feeling of fear, apprehension and worry often accompanied by physical sensations such as palpitations, chest pain and/or shortness of breath.
Z-score	A Z-score is a score that shows how many standard deviations above or below the mean a score.
Standard deviation	In probability and statistics, the standard deviation is the most commonly used measure of statistical dispersion. Simply put, it measures how spread out the values in a data set are.
Self-efficacy	Self-efficacy is the belief that one has the capabilities to execute the courses of actions required to manage prospective situations.
Affect	A subjective feeling or emotional tone often accompanied by bodily expressions noticeable to others is called affect.
Variable	A variable refers to a measurable factor, characteristic, or attribute of an individual or a system.
Postulates	Postulates are general statements about behavior that cannot be directly verified. They are used to generate theorems which can be tested.
Correlation	A statistical technique for determining the degree of association between two or more variables is referred to as correlation.
Emotion	An emotion is a mental states that arise spontaneously, rather than through conscious effort. They are often accompanied by physiological changes.
Perception	Perception is the process of acquiring, interpreting, selecting, and organizing sensory information.
Construct	A generalized concept, such as anxiety or gravity, is a construct.
Likert scale	A Likert scale is a type of psychometric scale often used in questionnaires. It asks respondents to specify their level of agreement to each of a list of statements. It is a bipolar scaling method, measuring either positive and negative response to a statement.
Individual differences	Individual differences psychology studies the ways in which individual people differ in their behavior. This is distinguished from other aspects of psychology in that although psychology is ostensibly a study of individuals, modern psychologists invariably study groups.
Nerve	A nerve is an enclosed, cable-like bundle of nerve fibers or axons, which includes the glia that ensheath the axons in myelin. Neurons are sometimes called nerve cells, though this term is technically imprecise since many neurons do not form nerves.
Personality	Personality refers to the pattern of enduring characteristics that differentiates a person, the patterns of behaviors that make each individual unique.
Drive Theory	Drive Theory states that due to the unpredictable nature of people, a person performing a task rarely knows for certain what others are going to do in response. This creates a state of arousal that in some cases will facilitate performance, while in other cases it will inhibit performance.
Drive reduction	Drive reduction theories are based on the need-state. Drive activates behavior. Reinforcement occurs whenever drive is reduced, leading to learning of whatever response solves the need. Thus the reduction in need serves as reinforcement and produces reinforcement of the response that leads to it.
Motivation	In psychology, motivation is the driving force (desire) behind all actions of an organism.
Innate	Innate behavior is not learned or influenced by the environment, rather, it is present or predisposed at birth.

Go to **Cram101.com** for the Practice Tests for this Chapter.

Individualistic	Cultures have been classified as individualistic, which means having a set of values that give priority to personal goals rather than group goals.
Qualitative research	Qualitative research is a broad term that describes research that focuses on how individuals and groups view and understand the world and construct meaning out of their experiences.
Theories	Theories are logically self-consistent models or frameworks describing the behavior of a certain natural or social phenomenon. They are broad explanations and predictions concerning phenomena of interest.

Anxiety	Anxiety is a complex combination of the feeling of fear, apprehension and worry often accompanied by physical sensations such as palpitations, chest pain and/or shortness of breath.
Hypothesis	A specific statement about behavior or mental processes that is testable through research is a hypothesis.
Stress management	Stress management encompasses techniques intended to equip a person with effective coping mechanisms for dealing with psychological stress.
Emotion	An emotion is a mental states that arise spontaneously, rather than through conscious effort. They are often accompanied by physiological changes.
Problem-focused coping	Lazarus' problem-focused coping is a strategy used by individuals who face their troubles and try to solve them.
Stimulus	A change in an environmental condition that elicits a response is a stimulus.
Emotion-focused coping	Lazarus' emotion-focused coping describes individuals' response to stress demonstrated in an emotional manner, especially using defensive methods.
Repression	A defense mechanism, repression involves moving thoughts unacceptable to the ego into the unconscious, where they cannot be easily accessed.
Graham	Graham has conducted a number of studies that reveal stronger socioeconomic-status influences rather than ethnic influences in achievement.
Survey	A method of scientific investigation in which a large sample of people answer questions about their attitudes or behavior is referred to as a survey.
Innate	Innate behavior is not learned or influenced by the environment, rather, it is present or predisposed at birth.
Applied research	Applied research is done to solve specific, practical questions; its primary aim is not to gain knowledge for its own sake. It can be exploratory but often it is descriptive. It is almost always done on the basis of basic research.
Learning	Learning is a relatively permanent change in behavior that results from experience. Thus, to attribute a behavioral change to learning, the change must be relatively permanent and must result from experience.
Correlation	A statistical technique for determining the degree of association between two or more variables is referred to as correlation.
Generalizability	The ability to extend a set of findings observed in one piece of research to other situations and groups is called generalizability.
Locus of control	The place to which an individual attributes control over the receiving of reinforcers -either inside or outside the self is referred to as locus of control.
Social support	Social Support is the physical and emotional comfort given by family, friends, co-workers and others. Research has identified three main types of social support: emotional, practical, sharing points of view.
Tunnel vision	Tunnel vision is a visual problem or symptom of another problem which produces loss of peripheral vision.
Meditation	Meditation usually refers to a state in which the body is consciously relaxed and the mind is allowed to become calm and focused.
Attention	Attention is the cognitive process of selectively concentrating on one thing while ignoring other things. Psychologists have labeled three types of attention: sustained attention,

selective attention, and divided attention.

Anxiety	Anxiety is a complex combination of the feeling of fear, apprehension and worry often accompanied by physical sensations such as palpitations, chest pain and/or shortness of breath.
Physiological changes	Alterations in heart rate, blood pressure, perspiration, and other involuntary responses are physiological changes.
Nervous system	The body's electrochemical communication circuitry, made up of billions of neurons is a nervous system.
Sympathetic	The sympathetic nervous system activates what is often termed the "fight or flight response". It is an automatic regulation system, that is, one that operates without the intervention of conscious thought.
Attention	Attention is the cognitive process of selectively concentrating on one thing while ignoring other things. Psychologists have labeled three types of attention: sustained attention, selective attention, and divided attention.
Perception	Perception is the process of acquiring, interpreting, selecting, and organizing sensory information.
Learning	Learning is a relatively permanent change in behavior that results from experience. Thus, to attribute a behavioral change to learning, the change must be relatively permanent and must result from experience.
Skeletal muscle	Skeletal muscle is a type of striated muscle, attached to the skeleton. They are used to facilitate movement, by applying force to bones and joints; via contraction. They generally contract voluntarily (via nerve stimulation), although they can contract involuntarily.
Stages	Stages represent relatively discrete periods of time in which functioning is qualitatively different from functioning at other periods.
Relaxation training	Relaxation training is an intervention technique used for tics. The person is taught to relax the muscles involved in the tics.
Autogenic training	Autogenic training is a term for a relaxation technique developed by the German psychiatrist Johannes Schultz. It usually involves a series of sessions in which the patients learn to relax their limbs, heart, and breathing. The goal is to induce a pleasant, warm feeling throughout most of the body but induce a feeling of coolness in the forehead. The technique is used against stress-induced psychosomatic disorders.
Hypnosis	Hypnosis is a psychological state whose existence and effects are strongly debated. Some believe that it is a state under which the subject's mind becomes so suggestible that the hypnotist, the one who induces the state, can establish communication with the subconscious mind of the subject and command behavior that the subject would not choose to perform in a conscious state.
Psychiatrist	A psychiatrist is a physician who specializes in the diagnosis and treatment of psychological disorders.
Sensation	Sensation is the first stage in the chain of biochemical and neurologic events that begins with the impinging of a stimulus upon the receptor cells of a sensory organ, which then leads to perception, the mental state that is reflected in statements like "I see a uniformly blue wall."
Anecdotal evidence	Anecdotal evidence is unreliable evidence based on personal experience that has not been empirically tested, and which is often used in an argument as if it had been scientifically or statistically proven. The person using anecdotal evidence may or may not be aware of the fact that, by doing so, they are generalizing.

Go to **Cram101.com** for the Practice Tests for this Chapter.

Meditation	Meditation usually refers to a state in which the body is consciously relaxed and the mind is allowed to become calm and focused.
Attitude	An enduring mental representation of a person, place, or thing that evokes an emotional response and related behavior is called attitude.
Mantra	A mantra is a religious syllable or poem, typically from the Sanskrit language. Their use varies according to the school and philosophy associated with the mantra. They are primarily used as spiritual conduits, words and vibrations that instill one-pointed concentration in the devotee..
Transcendental Meditation	The simplified form of meditation brought to the United States by the Maharishi Mahesh Yogi and used as a method for coping with stress is called transcendental meditation.
Autonomic nervous system	A division of the peripheral nervous system, the autonomic nervous system, regulates glands and activities such as heartbeat, respiration, digestion, and dilation of the pupils. It is responsible for homeostasis, maintaining a relatively constant internal environment .
Gross motor skills	Gross motor skills refer to motor skills that involve large muscle activities, such as walking.
Biofeedback	Biofeedback is the process of measuring and quantifying an aspect of a subject's physiology, analyzing the data, and then feeding back the information to the subject in a form that allows the subject to enact physiological change.
Chronic	Chronic refers to a relatively long duration, usually more than a few months.
Electroencep-alogram	Electroencephalography is the neurophysiologic measurement of the electrical activity of the brain by recording from electrodes placed on the scalp, or in the special cases on the cortex. The resulting traces are known as an electroencephalogram and represent so-called brainwaves.
Brain	The brain controls and coordinates most movement, behavior and homeostatic body functions such as heartbeat, blood pressure, fluid balance and body temperature. Functions of the brain are responsible for cognition, emotion, memory, motor learning and other sorts of learning. The brain is primarily made up of two types of cells: glia and neurons.
Beta wave	A low amplitude brain beta wave with multiple and varying frequencies is often associated with active, busy or anxious thinking and active concentration.
Alpha wave	The brain wave associated with deep relaxation is referred to as the alpha wave. Recorded by electroencephalography (EEG) , they are synchronous and coherent (regular like sawtooth) and in the frequency range of 8 - 12 Hz. It is also called Berger's wave in memory of the founder of EEG.
Laboratory setting	Research setting in which the behavior of interest does not naturally occur is called a laboratory setting.
Feedback	Feedback refers to information returned to a person about the effects a response has had.
Affect	A subjective feeling or emotional tone often accompanied by bodily expressions noticeable to others is called affect.
Clinician	A health professional authorized to provide services to people suffering from one or more pathologies is a clinician.
Selective attention	Selective attention is a type of attention which involves focusing on a specific aspect of a scene while ignoring other aspects.

Matching hypothesis	The matching hypothesis is a popular theory proposed by Walster in 1966, on what causes people to be attracted to their partners. It claims that people are more likely to form long term relationships with people who are roughly equally as physically attractive as themselves.
Hypothesis	A specific statement about behavior or mental processes that is testable through research is a hypothesis.
Affect	A subjective feeling or emotional tone often accompanied by bodily expressions noticeable to others is called affect.
Motivation	In psychology, motivation is the driving force (desire) behind all actions of an organism.
Reasoning	Reasoning is the act of using reason to derive a conclusion from certain premises. There are two main methods to reach a conclusion,deductive reasoning and inductive reasoning.
Reinforcement	In operant conditioning, reinforcement is any change in an environment that (a) occurs after the behavior, (b) seems to make that behavior re-occur more often in the future and (c) that reoccurence of behavior must be the result of the change.
Attention	Attention is the cognitive process of selectively concentrating on one thing while ignoring other things. Psychologists have labeled three types of attention: sustained attention, selective attention, and divided attention.
Anxiety	Anxiety is a complex combination of the feeling of fear, apprehension and worry often accompanied by physical sensations such as palpitations, chest pain and/or shortness of breath.
Acute	Acute means sudden, sharp, and abrupt. Usually short in duration.
Habit	A habit is a response that has become completely separated from its eliciting stimulus. Early learning theorists used the term to describe S-R associations, however not all S-R associations become a habit, rather many are extinguished after reinforcement is withdrawn.

Pitch	Pitch is the psychological interpretation of a sound or musical tone corresponding to its physical frequency
Control group	A group that does not receive the treatment effect in an experiment is referred to as the control group or sometimes as the comparison group.
Theories	Theories are logically self-consistent models or frameworks describing the behavior of a certain natural or social phenomenon. They are broad explanations and predictions concerning phenomena of interest.
Cognitive science	Cognitive Science is the scientific study of the mind and brain and how they give rise to behavior. The field is highly interdisciplinary and is closely related to several other areas, including psychology, artificial intelligence, linguistics and psycholinguistics, philosophy, neuroscience, logic, robotics, anthropology and biology.
Elaboration	The extensiveness of processing at any given level of memory is called elaboration. The use of elaboration changes developmentally. Adolescents are more likely to use elaboration spontaneously than children.
Fisher	Fisher was a eugenicist, evolutionary biologist, geneticist and statistician. He has been described as "The greatest of Darwin's successors", and a genius who almost single-handedly created the foundations for modern statistical science inventing the techniques of maximum likelihood and analysis of variance.
Brain	The brain controls and coordinates most movement, behavior and homeostatic body functions such as heartbeat, blood pressure, fluid balance and body temperature. Functions of the brain are responsible for cognition, emotion, memory, motor learning and other sorts of learning. The brain is primarily made up of two types of cells: glia and neurons.
Anxiety	Anxiety is a complex combination of the feeling of fear, apprehension and worry often accompanied by physical sensations such as palpitations, chest pain and/or shortness of breath.
Emotion	An emotion is a mental states that arise spontaneously, rather than through conscious effort. They are often accompanied by physiological changes.
Learning	Learning is a relatively permanent change in behavior that results from experience. Thus, to attribute a behavioral change to learning, the change must be relatively permanent and must result from experience.
Attention	Attention is the cognitive process of selectively concentrating on one thing while ignoring other things. Psychologists have labeled three types of attention: sustained attention, selective attention, and divided attention.
Schema	Schema refers to a way of mentally representing the world, such as a belief or an expectation, that can influence perception of persons, objects, and situations.
Senses	The senses are systems that consist of a sensory cell type that respond to a specific kind of physical energy, and that correspond to a defined region within the brain where the signals are received and interpreted.
Questionnaire	A self-report method of data collection or clinical assessment method in which the individual being studied checks off items on a printed list, answers multiple-choice questions, or writes out answers to essay questions aimed at producing a selfdescription is called questionnaire.
Individual differences	Individual differences psychology studies the ways in which individual people differ in their behavior. This is distinguished from other aspects of psychology in that although psychology is ostensibly a study of individuals, modern psychologists invariably study groups.

Go to **Cram101.com** for the Practice Tests for this Chapter.

Go to **Cram101.com** for the Practice Tests for this Chapter.
And, **NEVER** highlight a book again!

Cognition	The intellectual processes through which information is obtained, transformed, stored, retrieved, and otherwise used is cognition.
Cognitive restructuring	Cognitive restructuring refers to any behavior therapy procedure that attempts to alter the manner in which a client thinks about life so that he or she changes overt behavior and emotions.
Motivation	In psychology, motivation is the driving force (desire) behind all actions of an organism.
Relaxation training	Relaxation training is an intervention technique used for tics. The person is taught to relax the muscles involved in the tics.
Behavior rehearsal	A behavior therapy technique in which a client practices new behavior in the consulting room, often aided by demonstrations and role-play by the therapist is referred to as behavior rehearsal.
Desensitization	Desensitization refers to the type of sensory or behavioral adaptation in which we become less sensitive to constant stimuli.
Adaptation	Adaptation is a lowering of sensitivity to a stimulus following prolonged exposure to that stimulus. Behavioral adaptations are special ways a particular organism behaves to survive in its natural habitat.
Wolpe	Wolpe is best known for applying classical conditioning principles to the treatment of phobias, called systematic desensitization. Any "neutral" stimulus, simple or complex that happens to make an impact on an individual at about the time that a fear reaction is evoked acquires the ability to evoke fear subsequently. An acquired CS-CR relationship should be extinguishable.
Phobia	A persistent, irrational fear of an object, situation, or activity that the person feels compelled to avoid is referred to as a phobia.
Acquisition	Acquisition is the process of adapting to the environment, learning or becoming conditioned. In classical conditoning terms, it is the initial learning of the stimulus response link, which involves a neutral stimulus being associated with a unconditioned stimulus and becoming a conditioned stimulus.
Depression	In everyday language depression refers to any downturn in mood, which may be relatively transitory and perhaps due to something trivial. This is differentiated from Clinical depression which is marked by symptoms that last two weeks or more and are so severe that they interfere with daily living.
Stress inoculation	Use of positive coping statements to control fear and anxiety is a form of stress inoculation.
Self-instructional training	A cognitive-behavioral approach that tries to help people improve their overt behavior by changing how they silently talk to themselves is called self-instructional training.
Problem solving	An attempt to find an appropriate way of attaining a goal when the goal is not readily available is called problem solving.
In vitro	In vitro is an experimental technique where the experiment is performed in a test tube, or generally outside a living organism or cell.
Stages	Stages represent relatively discrete periods of time in which functioning is qualitatively different from functioning at other periods.
Stress management	Stress management encompasses techniques intended to equip a person with effective coping mechanisms for dealing with psychological stress.

Affect	A subjective feeling or emotional tone often accompanied by bodily expressions noticeable to others is called affect.
Tactile	Pertaining to the sense of touch is referred to as tactile.
Feedback	Feedback refers to information returned to a person about the effects a response has had.

Hypnosis	Hypnosis is a psychological state whose existence and effects are strongly debated. Some believe that it is a state under which the subject's mind becomes so suggestible that the hypnotist, the one who induces the state, can establish communication with the subconscious mind of the subject and command behavior that the subject would not choose to perform in a conscious state.
Anxiety	Anxiety is a complex combination of the feeling of fear, apprehension and worry often accompanied by physical sensations such as palpitations, chest pain and/or shortness of breath.
Emotion	An emotion is a mental states that arise spontaneously, rather than through conscious effort. They are often accompanied by physiological changes.
Autogenic training	Autogenic training is a term for a relaxation technique developed by the German psychiatrist Johannes Schultz. It usually involves a series of sessions in which the patients learn to relax their limbs, heart, and breathing. The goal is to induce a pleasant, warm feeling throughout most of the body but induce a feeling of coolness in the forehead. The technique is used against stress-induced psychosomatic disorders.
Meditation	Meditation usually refers to a state in which the body is consciously relaxed and the mind is allowed to become calm and focused.
Attention	Attention is the cognitive process of selectively concentrating on one thing while ignoring other things. Psychologists have labeled three types of attention: sustained attention, selective attention, and divided attention.
Case study	A carefully drawn biography that may be obtained through interviews, questionnaires, and psychological tests is called a case study.
Self-hypnosis	Self-hypnosis is a process by which an individual trains the subconscious mind to believe something, or systematically schematizes the person's own mental associations, usually for a given purpose. This is accomplished through repetitive, constant self-affirmations, and may be seen as a form of self-induced brainwashing.
Theories	Theories are logically self-consistent models or frameworks describing the behavior of a certain natural or social phenomenon. They are broad explanations and predictions concerning phenomena of interest.
Trait	An enduring personality characteristic that tends to lead to certain behaviors is called a trait. The term trait also means a genetically inherited feature of an organism.
Perception	Perception is the process of acquiring, interpreting, selecting, and organizing sensory information.
Sensation	Sensation is the first stage in the chain of biochemical and neurologic events that begins with the impinging of a stimulus upon the receptor cells of a sensory organ, which then leads to perception, the mental state that is reflected in statements like "I see a uniformly blue wall."
Altered state of consciousness	Altered state of consciousness refers to a mental state other than ordinary waking consciousness, such as sleep, meditation, hypnosis, or a drug-induced state.
Consciousness	The awareness of the sensations, thoughts, and feelings being experienced at a given moment is called consciousness.
Social-cognitive theory	Social-cognitive theory, a school of psychology in the behaviorist tradition, includes cognitive factors in the explanation and prediction of behavior. It is a cognitively oriented learning theory in with observational learning and person variables such as values and expectances.

Motivation	In psychology, motivation is the driving force (desire) behind all actions of an organism.
Attitude	An enduring mental representation of a person, place, or thing that evokes an emotional response and related behavior is called attitude.
Dissociation	Dissociation is a psychological state or condition in which certain thoughts, emotions, sensations, or memories are separated from the rest.
Hilgard	Hilgard made headlines as a pioneer in the scientific study of hypnosis. He and his wife, Josephine, established the Laboratory of Hypnosis Research at Stanford.
Brain	The brain controls and coordinates most movement, behavior and homeostatic body functions such as heartbeat, blood pressure, fluid balance and body temperature. Functions of the brain are responsible for cognition, emotion, memory, motor learning and other sorts of learning. The brain is primarily made up of two types of cells: glia and neurons.
Hidden observer	A part of consciousness that is aware of another part of consciousness is referred to as hidden observer.
Personality	Personality refers to the pattern of enduring characteristics that differentiates a person, the patterns of behaviors that make each individual unique.
Hallucination	A hallucination is a sensory perception experienced in the absence of an external stimulus, as distinct from an illusion, which is a misperception of an external stimulus. They may occur in any sensory modality - visual, auditory, olfactory, gustatory, tactile, or mixed.
Amnesia	Amnesia is a condition in which memory is disturbed. The causes of amnesia are organic or functional. Organic causes include damage to the brain, through trauma or disease, or use of certain (generally sedative) drugs.
Clinician	A health professional authorized to provide services to people suffering from one or more pathologies is a clinician.
Pitch	Pitch is the psychological interpretation of a sound or musical tone corresponding to its physical frequency
Re-experiencing	Careful and systematic visualizing and reliving of traumatic life events in order to diminish their power and emotional effects as a means of treating dissociative identity disorder or posttraumatic stress disorder is called re-experiencing.
Transcendental Meditation	The simplified form of meditation brought to the United States by the Maharishi Mahesh Yogi and used as a method for coping with stress is called transcendental meditation.
Fixation	Fixation in abnormal psychology is the state where an individual becomes obsessed with an attachment to another human, animal or inanimate object. Fixation in vision refers to maintaining the gaze in a constant direction. .

Hypnosis	Hypnosis is a psychological state whose existence and effects are strongly debated. Some believe that it is a state under which the subject's mind becomes so suggestible that the hypnotist, the one who induces the state, can establish communication with the subconscious mind of the subject and command behavior that the subject would not choose to perform in a conscious state.
Attention	Attention is the cognitive process of selectively concentrating on one thing while ignoring other things. Psychologists have labeled three types of attention: sustained attention, selective attention, and divided attention.
Learning	Learning is a relatively permanent change in behavior that results from experience. Thus, to attribute a behavioral change to learning, the change must be relatively permanent and must result from experience.
Anxiety	Anxiety is a complex combination of the feeling of fear, apprehension and worry often accompanied by physical sensations such as palpitations, chest pain and/or shortness of breath.
Control group	A group that does not receive the treatment effect in an experiment is referred to as the control group or sometimes as the comparison group.
Mayer	Mayer developed the concept of emotional intelligence with Peter Salovey. He is one of the authors of the Mayer-Salovey-Caruso Emotional Intelligence Test, and has developed a new, integrated framework for personality psychology, known as the Systems Framework for Pesronality Psychology.
Psychometric	Psychometric study is concerned with the theory and technique of psychological measurement, which includes the measurement of knowledge, abilities, attitudes, and personality traits. The field is primarily concerned with the study of differences between individuals
Reliability	Reliability means the extent to which a test produces a consistent , reproducible score .
Validity	The extent to which a test measures what it is intended to measure is called validity.
Achievement motivation	The psychological need in humans for success is called achievement motivation.
Motivation	In psychology, motivation is the driving force (desire) behind all actions of an organism.
Automaticity	The ability to process information with little or no effort is referred to as automaticity.
Self-hypnosis	Self-hypnosis is a process by which an individual trains the subconscious mind to believe something, or systematically schematizes the person's own mental associations, usually for a given purpose. This is accomplished through repetitive, constant self-affirmations, and may be seen as a form of self-induced brainwashing.
Perception	Perception is the process of acquiring, interpreting, selecting, and organizing sensory information.
Self-awareness	Realization that one's existence and functioning are separate from those of other people and things is called self-awareness.
Personality	Personality refers to the pattern of enduring characteristics that differentiates a person, the patterns of behaviors that make each individual unique.
Variable	A variable refers to a measurable factor, characteristic, or attribute of an individual or a system.
American Psychological Association	The American Psychological Association is a professional organization representing psychology in the US. The mission statement is to "advance psychology as a science and profession and as a means of promoting health, education , and human welfare".

Society	The social sciences use the term society to mean a group of people that form a semi-closed (or semi-open) social system, in which most interactions are with other individuals belonging to the group.
Innate	Innate behavior is not learned or influenced by the environment, rather, it is present or predisposed at birth.
Social psychology	Social psychology is the study of the nature and causes of human social behavior, with an emphasis on how people think towards each other and how they relate to each other.
Affect	A subjective feeling or emotional tone often accompanied by bodily expressions noticeable to others is called affect.

Go to **Cram101.com** for the Practice Tests for this Chapter.

Social psychology	Social psychology is the study of the nature and causes of human social behavior, with an emphasis on how people think towards each other and how they relate to each other.
Pitch	Pitch is the psychological interpretation of a sound or musical tone corresponding to its physical frequency
Attention	Attention is the cognitive process of selectively concentrating on one thing while ignoring other things. Psychologists have labeled three types of attention: sustained attention, selective attention, and divided attention.
Catharsis hypothesis	The view that opportunities to express anger and hostility in relatively safe ways will reduce a person's likelihood of engaging in more harmful forms of aggression is referred to as the catharsis hypothesis.
Hypothesis	A specific statement about behavior or mental processes that is testable through research is a hypothesis.
Catharsis	Catharsis has been adopted by modern psychotherapy as the act of giving expression to deep emotions often associated with events in the individuals past which have never before been adequately expressed.
Theories	Theories are logically self-consistent models or frameworks describing the behavior of a certain natural or social phenomenon. They are broad explanations and predictions concerning phenomena of interest.
Reinforcement	In operant conditioning, reinforcement is any change in an environment that (a) occurs after the behavior, (b) seems to make that behavior re-occur more often in the future and (c) that reoccurence of behavior must be the result of the change.
Moral reasoning	Moral reasoning involves concepts of justice, whereas social conventional judgments are concepts of social organization.
Reasoning	Reasoning is the act of using reason to derive a conclusion from certain premises. There are two main methods to reach a conclusion,deductive reasoning and inductive reasoning.
Assertiveness	Assertiveness basically means the ability to express your thoughts and feelings in a way that clearly states your needs and keeps the lines of communication open with the other.
Instinct theory	The notion that human behavior is motivated by certain innate tendencies, or instincts, shared by all individuals is an instinct theory.
Sigmund Freud	Sigmund Freud was the founder of the psychoanalytic school, based on his theory that unconscious motives control much behavior, that particular kinds of unconscious thoughts and memories are the source of neurosis, and that neurosis could be treated through bringing these unconscious thoughts and memories to consciousness in psychoanalytic treatment.
Instinct	Instinct is the word used to describe inherent dispositions towards particular actions. They are generally an inherited pattern of responses or reactions to certain kinds of situations.
Lorenz	Lorenz demonstrated how incubator-hatched geese would imprint on the first suitable moving stimulus they saw within what he called a "critical period" of about 36 hours shortly after hatching. Most famously, the goslings would imprint on Lorenz himself .
Innate	Innate behavior is not learned or influenced by the environment, rather, it is present or predisposed at birth.
Society	The social sciences use the term society to mean a group of people that form a semi-closed (or semi-open) social system, in which most interactions are with other individuals belonging to the group.
Social learning	Social learning theory explains the process of gender typing in terms of observation,

Go to **Cram101.com** for the Practice Tests for this Chapter.

theory	imitation, and role playing .
Social learning	Social learning is learning that occurs as a function of observing, retaining and replicating behavior observed in others. Although social learning can occur at any stage in life, it is thought to be particularly important during childhood, particularly as authority becomes important.
Learning	Learning is a relatively permanent change in behavior that results from experience. Thus, to attribute a behavioral change to learning, the change must be relatively permanent and must result from experience.
Bandura	Bandura is best known for his work on social learning theory or Social Cognitivism. His famous Bobo doll experiment illustrated that people learn from observing others.
Modeling	A type of behavior learned through observation of others demonstrating the same behavior is modeling.
Role model	A person who serves as a positive example of desirable behavior is referred to as a role model.
Cognitive development	The process by which a child's understanding of the world changes as a function of age and experience is called cognitive development.
Piaget	Piaget argued that young children's answers were qualitatively different than older children rather than quantitative. There are two major aspects to his theory: the process of coming to know and the stages we move through as we gradually acquire this ability.
Moral development	Development regarding rules and conventions about what people should do in their interactions with other people is called moral development.
Sears	Sears focused on the application of the social learning theory (SLT) to socialization processes, and how children internalize the values, attitudes, and behaviors predominant in their culture. He articulated the place of parents in fostering internalization. In addition, he was among the first social learning theorists to officially acknowledge the reciprocal interaction on an individual's behavior and their environment
Affect	A subjective feeling or emotional tone often accompanied by bodily expressions noticeable to others is called affect.
Depression	In everyday language depression refers to any downturn in mood, which may be relatively transitory and perhaps due to something trivial. This is differentiated from Clinical depression which is marked by symptoms that last two weeks or more and are so severe that they interfere with daily living.
Incentive	An incentive is what is expected once a behavior is performed. An incentive acts as a reinforcer.
Questionnaire	A self-report method of data collection or clinical assessment method in which the individual being studied checks off items on a printed list, answers multiple-choice questions, or writes out answers to essay questions aimed at producing a selfdescription is called questionnaire.
Trait	An enduring personality characteristic that tends to lead to certain behaviors is called a trait. The term trait also means a genetically inherited feature of an organism.
Wisdom	Wisdom is the ability to make correct judgments and decisions. It is an intangible quality gained through experience. Whether or not something is wise is determined in a pragmatic sense by its popularity, how long it has been around, and its ability to predict against future events.
Variable	A variable refers to a measurable factor, characteristic, or attribute of an individual or a

	system.
Social comparison	Social comparison theory is the idea that individuals learn about and assess themselves by comparison with other people. Research shows that individuals tend to lean more toward social comparisons in situations that are ambiguous.
Ego	In Freud's view the Ego serves to balance our primitive needs and our moral beliefs and taboos. Relying on experience, a healthy Ego provides the ability to adapt to reality and interact with the outside world.
Attitude	An enduring mental representation of a person, place, or thing that evokes an emotional response and related behavior is called attitude.
Punishment	Punishment is the addtion of a stimulus that reduces the frequency of a response, or the removal of a stimulus that results in a reduction of the response.
Alcoholic	An alcoholic is dependent on alcohol as characterized by craving, loss of control, physical dependence and withdrawal symptoms, and tolerance.
False consensus effect	The false consensus effect refers to the tendency for people to overestimate the degree to which others agree with them.
Infatuation	The term "infatuation" carries connotations of immaturity or fatuousness, while "limerence" is intended to separate these connotations from the emotion.

99

Social facilitation	Social facilitation refers to the process by which a person's performance is increased when other members of a group engage in similar behavior.
Social psychology	Social psychology is the study of the nature and causes of human social behavior, with an emphasis on how people think towards each other and how they relate to each other.
Variable	A variable refers to a measurable factor, characteristic, or attribute of an individual or a system.
Zajonc	Zajonc is best known for his decades of work on the mere exposure effect, the phenomenon that repeated exposure to a stimulus brings about an attitude change in relation to the stimulus.
Perception	Perception is the process of acquiring, interpreting, selecting, and organizing sensory information.
Drive Theory	Drive Theory states that due to the unpredictable nature of people, a person performing a task rarely knows for certain what others are going to do in response. This creates a state of arousal that in some cases will facilitate performance, while in other cases it will inhibit performance.
Hypothesis	A specific statement about behavior or mental processes that is testable through research is a hypothesis.
Blocking	If the one of the two members of a compound stimulus fails to produce the CR due to an earlier conditioning of the other member of the compound stimulus, blocking has occurred.
Self-awareness	Realization that one's existence and functioning are separate from those of other people and things is called self-awareness.
Statistics	Statistics is a type of data analysis which practice includes the planning, summarizing, and interpreting of observations of a system possibly followed by predicting or forecasting of future events based on a mathematical model of the system being observed.
Statistic	A statistic is an observable random variable of a sample.

Social psychology	Social psychology is the study of the nature and causes of human social behavior, with an emphasis on how people think towards each other and how they relate to each other.
Group dynamics	The term group dynamics implies that individual behaviors may differ depending on individuals' current or prospective connections to a sociological group.
Social Cohesion	Social Cohesion is a state in society where the vast majority of citizens respect the law and one another's human rights. To achieve Social Cohesion is one of the two functions of the law, the second fuction being to achieve social progress.
Clique	A clique is an informal and restricted social group formed by a number of people who share common. Social roles vary, but two roles commonly associated with a female clique is notably applicable to most - that of the "queen bee" and that of the "outcast".
Construct	A generalized concept, such as anxiety or gravity, is a construct.
Perception	Perception is the process of acquiring, interpreting, selecting, and organizing sensory information.
Questionnaire	A self-report method of data collection or clinical assessment method in which the individual being studied checks off items on a printed list, answers multiple-choice questions, or writes out answers to essay questions aimed at producing a selfdescription is called questionnaire.
Cohesiveness	Cohesiveness with respect to conformity is the degree of attraction felt by an individual toward an influencing group.
Likert scale	A Likert scale is a type of psychometric scale often used in questionnaires. It asks respondents to specify their level of agreement to each of a list of statements. It is a bipolar scaling method, measuring either positive and negative response to a statement.
Antecedents	In behavior modification, events that typically precede the target response are called antecedents.
Dichotomy	A dichotomy is the division of a proposition into two parts which are both mutually exclusive – i.e. both cannot be simultaneously true – and jointly exhaustive – i.e. they cover the full range of possible outcomes. They are often contrasting and spoken of as "opposites".
Halo effect	The halo effect occurs when a person's positive or negative traits seem to "spill over" from one area of their personality to another in others' perceptions of them.
Research design	A research design tests a hypothesis. The basic typess are: descriptive, correlational, and experimental.
Meta-analysis	In statistics, a meta-analysis combines the results of several studies that address a set of related research hypotheses.
Self-efficacy	Self-efficacy is the belief that one has the capabilities to execute the courses of actions required to manage prospective situations.
Self-esteem	Self-esteem refers to a person's subjective appraisal of himself or herself as intrinsically positive or negative to some degree.
Trait	An enduring personality characteristic that tends to lead to certain behaviors is called a trait. The term trait also means a genetically inherited feature of an organism.
Stages	Stages represent relatively discrete periods of time in which functioning is qualitatively different from functioning at other periods.
Norms	In testing, standards of test performance that permit the comparison of one person's score on the test to the scores of others who have taken the same test are referred to as norms.

Go to **Cram101.com** for the Practice Tests for this Chapter.

Self-worth	In psychology, self-esteem or self-worth refers to a person's subjective appraisal of himself or herself as intrinsically positive or negative to some degree.
Conformity	Conformity is the degree to which members of a group will change their behavior, views and attitudes to fit the views of the group. The group can influence members via unconscious processes or via overt social pressure on individuals.
Interpersonal attraction	Interpersonal attraction is the attraction between people which leads to friendships and romantic relationships. Major variables include propinquity, similarity, familiarity, reciprocal liking, and physical attractiveness.
Personal prejudice	Prejudicial attitudes held toward persons who are perceived as a direct threat to one's own interests is called a personal prejudice.
Prejudice	Prejudice in general, implies coming to a judgment on the subject before learning where the preponderance of the evidence actually lies, or formation of a judgement without direct experience.
Affect	A subjective feeling or emotional tone often accompanied by bodily expressions noticeable to others is called affect.
Variable	A variable refers to a measurable factor, characteristic, or attribute of an individual or a system.

Initiating structure	Initiating structure is a leadership style that is characterized by a concern with task accomplishment.
Propinquity	In social psychology, propinquity is one of the main factors leading to interpersonal attraction. It refers to the physical or psychological proximity between people.
Motivation	In psychology, motivation is the driving force (desire) behind all actions of an organism.
Path-goal	In organizational studies, the path-goal model of leadership states that a leader's function is to clear the path toward the goal of the group, by meeting the needs of subordinates. The model was developed jointly by Martin Evans and Robert House.
Theories	Theories are logically self-consistent models or frameworks describing the behavior of a certain natural or social phenomenon. They are broad explanations and predictions concerning phenomena of interest.
Fiedler	The Fiedler contingency model is a leadership theory of Industrial and Organizational Psychology. It postulates that the leader's effectiveness is based on 'situational contingency', that is a result of interaction of two factors, known as leadership style and situational favorableness.
Trait	An enduring personality characteristic that tends to lead to certain behaviors is called a trait. The term trait also means a genetically inherited feature of an organism.
Evolution	Commonly used to refer to gradual change, evolution is the change in the frequency of alleles within a population from one generation to the next. This change may be caused by different mechanisms, including natural selection, genetic drift, or changes in population (gene flow).
Personality	Personality refers to the pattern of enduring characteristics that differentiates a person, the patterns of behaviors that make each individual unique.
Social psychology	Social psychology is the study of the nature and causes of human social behavior, with an emphasis on how people think towards each other and how they relate to each other.
Scheme	According to Piaget, a hypothetical mental structure that permits the classification and organization of new information is called a scheme.
Hypothesis	A specific statement about behavior or mental processes that is testable through research is a hypothesis.
A priori	The term A Priori is considered to mean propositional knowledge that can be had without, or "prior to", experience.
Personality test	A personality test aims to describe aspects of a person's character that remain stable across situations.
Trait theory	According to trait theory, personality can be broken down into a limited number of traits, which are present in each individual to a greater or lesser degree. This approach is highly compatible with the quantitative psychometric approach to personality testing.
Personality inventory	A self-report questionnaire by which an examinee indicates whether statements assessing habitual tendencies apply to him or her is referred to as a personality inventory.
Personality trait	According to the Diagnostic and Statistical Manual of the American Psychiatric Association, a personality trait is a "prominent aspect of personality that is exhibited in a wide range of important social and personal contexts. ...".
Friendship	The essentials of friendship are reciprocity and commitment between individuals who see themselves more or less as equals. Interaction between friends rests on a more equal power base than the interaction between children and adults.
Construct	A generalized concept, such as anxiety or gravity, is a construct.

Go to **Cram101.com** for the Practice Tests for this Chapter.

Contingency Theory	The Contingency Theory of Classical Conditioning disagreed on what made a CS a useful predictor. It was more than the number of CS-US pairings, rather, it was the contingency between the CS and US.
Least preferred co-worker	Fiedler measured the personality of the leader by the least preferred co-worker scale. The scale asks a leader to think of all the persons with whom he or she has ever worked, and then to describe the one person with whom he or she worked the least well with.
Personality type	A persistent style of complex behaviors defined by a group of related traits is referred to as a personality type. Myer Friedman and his co-workers first defined personality types in the 1950s. Friedman classified people into 2 categories, Type A and Type B.
Empathy	Empathy is the recognition and understanding of the states of mind, including beliefs, desires and particularly emotions of others without injecting your own.
Leader-member exchange theory	Leader-member exchange theory views leadership from the perspective of individual leader-subordinate pairs.
Exchange theory	A relationship in which the participants expect and desire strict reciprocity in their interactions is referred to as exchange theory.
Norms	In testing, standards of test performance that permit the comparison of one person's score on the test to the scores of others who have taken the same test are referred to as norms.
Tics	Tics are a repeated, impulsive action, almost reflexive in nature, which the person feels powerless to control or avoid.
Perception	Perception is the process of acquiring, interpreting, selecting, and organizing sensory information.
Attitude	An enduring mental representation of a person, place, or thing that evokes an emotional response and related behavior is called attitude.
Variable	A variable refers to a measurable factor, characteristic, or attribute of an individual or a system.
Paradigm	Paradigm refers to the set of practices that defines a scientific discipline during a particular period of time. It provides a framework from which to conduct research, it ensures that a certain range of phenomena, those on which the paradigm focuses, are explored thoroughly. Itmay also blind scientists to other, perhaps more fruitful, ways of dealing with their subject matter.
Anxiety	Anxiety is a complex combination of the feeling of fear, apprehension and worry often accompanied by physical sensations such as palpitations, chest pain and/or shortness of breath.
Questionnaire	A self-report method of data collection or clinical assessment method in which the individual being studied checks off items on a printed list, answers multiple-choice questions, or writes out answers to essay questions aimed at producing a selfdescription is called questionnaire.
Feedback	Feedback refers to information returned to a person about the effects a response has had.
Self-esteem	Self-esteem refers to a person's subjective appraisal of himself or herself as intrinsically positive or negative to some degree.
Assertiveness training	In behavior therapy, a direct method of training people to express their own desires and feelings and to maintain their own rights in interactions with others, while at the same time respecting the others' rights is called assertiveness training.
Assertiveness	Assertiveness basically means the ability to express your thoughts and feelings in a way that

Go to **Cram101.com** for the Practice Tests for this Chapter.

	clearly states your needs and keeps the lines of communication open with the other.
Attention	Attention is the cognitive process of selectively concentrating on one thing while ignoring other things. Psychologists have labeled three types of attention: sustained attention, selective attention, and divided attention.
Pitch	Pitch is the psychological interpretation of a sound or musical tone corresponding to its physical frequency
Ethnicity	Ethnicity refers to a characteristic based on cultural heritage, nationality characteristics, race, religion, and language.
Schema	Schema refers to a way of mentally representing the world, such as a belief or an expectation, that can influence perception of persons, objects, and situations.
Interdependence	Interdependence is a dynamic of being mutually responsible to and dependent on others.

Cholesterol	Cholesterol is a steroid, a lipid, and an alcohol, found in the cell membranes of all body tissues, and transported in the blood plasma of all animals. Cholesterol is an important component of the membranes of cells, providing stability; it makes the membrane's fluidity stable over a bigger temperature interval.
Sedentary lifestyle	Sedentary lifestyle is a type of lifestyle common in modern (particularly Western) civilizations, which is characterized by sitting most of the day (for example, in an office or at home). It is believed to be a factor in obesity and other disorders.
Population	Population refers to all members of a well-defined group of organisms, events, or things.
Diabetes	Diabetes is a medical disorder characterized by varying or persistent elevated blood sugar levels, especially after eating. All types of diabetes share similar symptoms and complications at advanced stages: dehydration and ketoacidosis, cardiovascular disease, chronic renal failure, retinal damage which can lead to blindness, nerve damage which can lead to erectile dysfunction, gangrene with risk of amputation of toes, feet, and even legs.
Affect	A subjective feeling or emotional tone often accompanied by bodily expressions noticeable to others is called affect.
Self-efficacy	Self-efficacy is the belief that one has the capabilities to execute the courses of actions required to manage prospective situations.
Depression	In everyday language depression refers to any downturn in mood, which may be relatively transitory and perhaps due to something trivial. This is differentiated from Clinical depression which is marked by symptoms that last two weeks or more and are so severe that they interfere with daily living.
Anxiety	Anxiety is a complex combination of the feeling of fear, apprehension and worry often accompanied by physical sensations such as palpitations, chest pain and/or shortness of breath.
Antidepressant	An antidepressant is a medication used primarily in the treatment of clinical depression. They are not thought to produce tolerance, although sudden withdrawal may produce adverse effects. They create little if any immediate change in mood and require between several days and several weeks to take effect.
Psychotherapy	Psychotherapy is a set of techniques based on psychological principles intended to improve mental health, emotional or behavioral issues.
Chronic	Chronic refers to a relatively long duration, usually more than a few months.
Acute	Acute means sudden, sharp, and abrupt. Usually short in duration.
Aerobic exercise	Aerobic exercise is a type of exercise in which muscles draw on oxygen in the blood as well as fats and glucose, that increase cardiovascular endurance.
Individual differences	Individual differences psychology studies the ways in which individual people differ in their behavior. This is distinguished from other aspects of psychology in that although psychology is ostensibly a study of individuals, modern psychologists invariably study groups.
Habit	A habit is a response that has become completely separated from its eliciting stimulus. Early learning theorists used the term to describe S-R associations, however not all S-R associations become a habit, rather many are extinguished after reinforcement is withdrawn.
Psychological disorder	Mental processes and/or behavior patterns that cause emotional distress and/or substantial impairment in functioning is a psychological disorder.
Clinical depression	Although nearly any mood with some element of sadness may colloquially be termed a depression, clinical depression is more than just a temporary state of sadness. Symptoms lasting two weeks or longer in duration, and of a severity that they begin to interfere with

Go to **Cram101.com** for the Practice Tests for this Chapter.

	daily living.
Meta-analysis	In statistics, a meta-analysis combines the results of several studies that address a set of related research hypotheses.
Schizophrenia	Schizophrenia is characterized by persistent defects in the perception or expression of reality. A person suffering from untreated schizophrenia typically demonstrates grossly disorganized thinking, and may also experience delusions or auditory hallucinations
Sleep patterns	The order and timing of daily sleep and waking periods are called sleep patterns.
Hallucination	A hallucination is a sensory perception experienced in the absence of an external stimulus, as distinct from an illusion, which is a misperception of an external stimulus. They may occur in any sensory modality - visual, auditory, olfactory, gustatory, tactile, or mixed.
Panic disorder	A panic attack is a period of intense fear or discomfort, typically with an abrupt onset and usually lasting no more than thirty minutes. The disorder is strikingly different from other types of anxiety, in that panic attacks are very sudden, appear to be unprovoked, and are often disabling. People who have repeated attacks, or feel severe anxiety about having another attack are said to have panic disorder.
Panic attack	An attack of overwhelming anxiety, fear, or terror is called panic attack.
Attitude	An enduring mental representation of a person, place, or thing that evokes an emotional response and related behavior is called attitude.
Perception	Perception is the process of acquiring, interpreting, selecting, and organizing sensory information.
Variable	A variable refers to a measurable factor, characteristic, or attribute of an individual or a system.
Learning	Learning is a relatively permanent change in behavior that results from experience. Thus, to attribute a behavioral change to learning, the change must be relatively permanent and must result from experience.
Hypothesis	A specific statement about behavior or mental processes that is testable through research is a hypothesis.
Premise	A premise is a statement presumed true within the context of a discourse, especially of a logical argument.
Meditation	Meditation usually refers to a state in which the body is consciously relaxed and the mind is allowed to become calm and focused.
Neurotransmitter	A neurotransmitter is a chemical that is used to relay, amplify and modulate electrical signals between a neurons and another cell.
Nerve	A nerve is an enclosed, cable-like bundle of nerve fibers or axons, which includes the glia that ensheath the axons in myelin. Neurons are sometimes called nerve cells, though this term is technically imprecise since many neurons do not form nerves.
Norepinephrine	Norepinephrine is released from the adrenal glands as a hormone into the blood, but it is also a neurotransmitter in the nervous system. As a stress hormone, it affects parts of the human brain where attention and impulsivity are controlled. Along with epinephrine, this compound effects the fight-or-flight response, activating the sympathetic nervous system to directly increase heart rate, release energy from fat, and increase muscle readiness.
Serotonin	Serotonin, a neurotransmitter, is believed to play an important part of the biochemistry of depression, bipolar disorder and anxiety. It is also believed to be influential on sexuality and appetite.

Dopamine	Dopamine is critical to the way the brain controls our movements and is a crucial part of the basal ganglia motor loop. It is commonly associated with the 'pleasure system' of the brain, providing feelings of enjoyment and reinforcement to motivate us to do, or continue doing, certain activities.
Brain	The brain controls and coordinates most movement, behavior and homeostatic body functions such as heartbeat, blood pressure, fluid balance and body temperature. Functions of the brain are responsible for cognition, emotion, memory, motor learning and other sorts of learning. The brain is primarily made up of two types of cells: glia and neurons.
Postulates	Postulates are general statements about behavior that cannot be directly verified. They are used to generate theorems which can be tested.
Endorphin	An endorphin is an endogenous opioid biochemical compound. They are peptides produced by the pituitary gland and the hypothalamus, and they resemble the opiates in their abilities to produce analgesia and a sense of well-being. In other words, they work as "natural pain killers."
Morphine	Morphine, the principal active agent in opium, is a powerful opioid analgesic drug. According to recent research, it may also be produced naturally by the human brain. Morphine is usually highly addictive, and tolerance and physical and psychological dependence develop quickly.
Positive relationship	Statistically, a positive relationship refers to a mathematical relationship in which increases in one measure are matched by increases in the other.
Socioeconomic Status	A family's socioeconomic status is based on family income, parental education level, parental occupation, and social status in the community. Those with high status often have more success in preparing their children for school because they have access to a wide range of resources.
Socioeconomic	Socioeconomic pertains to the study of the social and economic impacts of any product or service offering, market intervention or other activity on an economy as a whole and on the companies, organization and individuals who are its main economic actors.
Statistics	Statistics is a type of data analysis which practice includes the planning, summarizing, and interpreting of observations of a system possibly followed by predicting or forecasting of future events based on a mathematical model of the system being observed.
Statistic	A statistic is an observable random variable of a sample.
Motivation	In psychology, motivation is the driving force (desire) behind all actions of an organism.
Theories	Theories are logically self-consistent models or frameworks describing the behavior of a certain natural or social phenomenon. They are broad explanations and predictions concerning phenomena of interest.
Social norm	A social norm, is a rule that is socially enforced. In social situations, such as meetings, they are unwritten and often unstated rules that govern individuals' behavior. A social norm is most evident when not followed or broken.
Norms	In testing, standards of test performance that permit the comparison of one person's score on the test to the scores of others who have taken the same test are referred to as norms.
Theory of planned behavior	The theory of planned behavior links attitudes and behavior. It holds that human action is guided by three kinds of considerations: Beliefs about the likely outcomes of the behavior and the evaluations of these outcomes; Beliefs about the normative expectations of others and motivation to comply with these expectations; and, Beliefs about the presence of factors that may facilitate or impede performance of the behavior and the perceived power of these factors.

Go to **Cram101.com** for the Practice Tests for this Chapter.

Behavioral control	Behavioral control refers to the contingencies that determine the expression of a behavior through manipulations of reinforcement and punishment.
Schematic representation	The representation of objects in terms of real or potential interactions with other objects is called a schematic representation.
Stages	Stages represent relatively discrete periods of time in which functioning is qualitatively different from functioning at other periods.
Social cognitive theory	Social cognitive theory defines human behavior as a triadic, dynamic, and reciprocal interaction of personal factors, behavior, and the environment. Response consequences of a behavior are used to form expectations of behavioral outcomes. It is the ability to form these expectations that give humans the capability to predict the outcomes of their behavior, before the behavior is performed.
Stress inoculation	Use of positive coping statements to control fear and anxiety is a form of stress inoculation.
Autonomic nervous system	A division of the peripheral nervous system, the autonomic nervous system, regulates glands and activities such as heartbeat, respiration, digestion, and dilation of the pupils. It is responsible for homeostasis, maintaining a relatively constant internal environment .
Nervous system	The body's electrochemical communication circuitry, made up of billions of neurons is a nervous system.
Adaptation	Adaptation is a lowering of sensitivity to a stimulus following prolonged exposure to that stimulus. Behavioral adaptations are special ways a particular organism behaves to survive in its natural habitat.
Survey	A method of scientific investigation in which a large sample of people answer questions about their attitudes or behavior is referred to as a survey.
Personality	Personality refers to the pattern of enduring characteristics that differentiates a person, the patterns of behaviors that make each individual unique.
Longitudinal study	Longitudinal study is a type of developmental study in which the same group of participants is followed and measured for an extended period of time, often years.
Social psychology	Social psychology is the study of the nature and causes of human social behavior, with an emphasis on how people think towards each other and how they relate to each other.
Hypertension	Hypertension is a medical condition where the blood pressure in the arteries is chronically elevated. Persistent hypertension is one of the risk factors for strokes, heart attacks, heart failure and arterial aneurysm, and is a leading cause of chronic renal failure.
Shyness	A tendency to avoid others plus uneasiness and strain when socializing is called shyness.
Immune system	The most important function of the human immune system occurs at the cellular level of the blood and tissues. The lymphatic and blood circulation systems are highways for specialized white blood cells. These cells include B cells, T cells, natural killer cells, and macrophages. All function with the primary objective of recognizing, attacking and destroying bacteria, viruses, cancer cells, and all substances seen as foreign.
Suppression	Suppression is the defense mechanism where a memory is deliberately forgotten.
Sullivan	Sullivan developed the Self System, a configuration of the personality traits developed in childhood and reinforced by positive affirmation and the security operations developed in childhood to avoid anxiety and threats to self-esteem.
Human immunodefici-	The human immunodeficiency virus is a retrovirus that primarily infects vital components of the human immune system. It is transmitted through penetrative and oral sex; blood

Go to **Cram101.com** for the Practice Tests for this Chapter.

ncy virus	transfusion; the sharing of contaminated needles in health care settings and through drug injection; and, between mother and infant, during pregnancy, childbirth and breastfeeding.
Acquired immune deficiency syndrome	Acquired Immune Deficiency Syndrome is defined as a collection of symptoms and infections resulting from the depletion of the immune system caused by infection with the human immunodeficiency virus, commonly called HIV.
Asymptomatic	A disease is asymptomatic when it is at a stage where the patient does not experience symptoms. By their nature, asymptomatic diseases are not usually discovered until the patient undergoes medical tests (X-rays or other investigations). Some diseases remain asymptomatic for a remarkably long time, including some forms of cancer.
Syndrome	The term syndrome is the association of several clinically recognizable features, signs, symptoms, phenomena or characteristics which often occur together, so that the presence of one feature indicates the presence of the others.
Control group	A group that does not receive the treatment effect in an experiment is referred to as the control group or sometimes as the comparison group.
Lymphocyte	A lymphocyte is a type of white blood cell involved in the human body's immune system. There are two broad categories, namely T cells and B cells. The lymphocyte play an important and integral part of the body's defenses.
Leukocytes	Leukocytes are a component of blood. They help to defend the body against infectious disease and foreign materials as part of the immune system.
Self-concept	Self-concept refers to domain-specific evaluations of the self where a domain may be academics, athletics, etc.
Body image	A person's body image is their perception of their physical appearance. It is more than what a person thinks they will see in a mirror, it is inextricably tied to their self-esteem and acceptance by peers.
Construct	A generalized concept, such as anxiety or gravity, is a construct.
Physical attractiveness	Physical attractiveness is the perception of an individual as physically beautiful by other people.
Self-esteem	Self-esteem refers to a person's subjective appraisal of himself or herself as intrinsically positive or negative to some degree.
Self-worth	In psychology, self-esteem or self-worth refers to a person's subjective appraisal of himself or herself as intrinsically positive or negative to some degree.
Conditioning	Conditioning describes the process by which behaviors can be learned or modified through interaction with the environment.
Addiction	Addiction is an uncontrollable compulsion to repeat a behavior regardless of its consequences. Many drugs or behaviors can precipitate a pattern of conditions recognized as addiction, which include a craving for more of the drug or behavior, increased physiological tolerance to exposure, and withdrawal symptoms in the absence of the stimulus.
Normative	The term normative is used to describe the effects of those structures of culture which regulate the function of social activity.
Eating disorders	Psychological disorders characterized by distortion of the body image and gross disturbances in eating patterns are called eating disorders.
Anorexia nervosa	Anorexia nervosa is an eating disorder characterized by voluntary starvation and exercise stress.
Attention	Attention is the cognitive process of selectively concentrating on one thing while ignoring

other things. Psychologists have labeled three types of attention: sustained attention, selective attention, and divided attention.

Anorexia	Anorexia nervosa is an eating disorder characterized by voluntary starvation and exercise stress.
Binge	Binge refers to relatively brief episode of uncontrolled, excessive consumption.
Bulimia	Bulimia refers to a disorder in which a person binges on incredibly large quantities of food, then purges by vomiting or by using laxatives. Bulimia is often less about food, and more to do with deep psychological issues and profound feelings of lack of control.
Diagnostic and Statistical Manual of Mental Disorders	The Diagnostic and Statistical Manual of Mental Disorders, published by the American Psychiatric Association, is the handbook used most often in diagnosing mental disorders in the United States and internationally.
Mental disorder	Mental disorder refers to a disturbance in a person's emotions, drives, thought processes, or behavior that involves serious and relatively prolonged distress and/or impairment in ability to function, is not simply a normal response to some event or set of events in the person's environment.
Mental illness	Mental illness is the term formerly used to mean psychological disorder but less preferred because it implies that the causes of the disorder can be found in a medical disease process.
Chemical imbalance	Chemical imbalance refers to relative excess or deficit in brain chemicals, such as neurotransmitters, that may be implicated in some psychological disorders.
Society	The social sciences use the term society to mean a group of people that form a semi-closed (or semi-open) social system, in which most interactions are with other individuals belonging to the group.
Anabolic steroid	Anabolic steroids are a class of natural and synthetic steroid hormones that promote cell growth and division, resulting in growth of muscle tissue and sometimes bone size and strength. Testosterone is the best known natural anabolic steroid, as well as the best known natural androgen.
Steroid	A steroid is a lipid characterized by a carbon skeleton with four fused rings. Different steroids vary in the functional groups attached to these rings. Hundreds of distinct steroids have been identified in plants and animals. Their most important role in most living systems is as hormones.
Short-term memory	Short-term memory is that part of memory which stores a limited amount of information for a limited amount of time (roughly 30-45 seconds). The second key concept associated with a short-term memory is that it has a finite capacity.
Intrinsic motivation	Intrinsic motivation causes people to engage in an activity for its own sake. They are subjective factors and include self-determination, curiosity, challenge, effort, and others.
Social support	Social Support is the physical and emotional comfort given by family, friends, co-workers and others. Research has identified three main types of social support: emotional, practical, sharing points of view.
Baseline	Measure of a particular behavior or process taken before the introduction of the independent variable or treatment is called the baseline.
Stage theory	Stage theory characterizes development by hypothesizing the existence of distinct, and often critical, periods of life. Each period follows one another in an orderly sequence.

Immune system	The most important function of the human immune system occurs at the cellular level of the blood and tissues. The lymphatic and blood circulation systems are highways for specialized white blood cells. These cells include B cells, T cells, natural killer cells, and macrophages. All function with the primary objective of recognizing, attacking and destroying bacteria, viruses, cancer cells, and all substances seen as foreign.
Syndrome	The term syndrome is the association of several clinically recognizable features, signs, symptoms, phenomena or characteristics which often occur together, so that the presence of one feature indicates the presence of the others.
Maladaptive	In psychology, a behavior or trait is adaptive when it helps an individual adjust and function well within their social environment. A maladaptive behavior or trait is counterproductive to the individual.
Adaptation	Adaptation is a lowering of sensitivity to a stimulus following prolonged exposure to that stimulus. Behavioral adaptations are special ways a particular organism behaves to survive in its natural habitat.
Cognitive appraisal	Lazarus' term for individuals' interpretation of events in their lives as threatening, harmful, or challenging and their determination of whether they have the resources to effectively cope with the events is referred to as cognitive appraisal.
Depression	In everyday language depression refers to any downturn in mood, which may be relatively transitory and perhaps due to something trivial. This is differentiated from Clinical depression which is marked by symptoms that last two weeks or more and are so severe that they interfere with daily living.
Insomnia	Insomnia is a sleep disorder characterized by an inability to sleep and/or to remain asleep for a reasonable period during the night.
Anxiety	Anxiety is a complex combination of the feeling of fear, apprehension and worry often accompanied by physical sensations such as palpitations, chest pain and/or shortness of breath.
Affective	Affective is the way people react emotionally, their ability to feel another living thing's pain or joy.
Perception	Perception is the process of acquiring, interpreting, selecting, and organizing sensory information.
Stages	Stages represent relatively discrete periods of time in which functioning is qualitatively different from functioning at other periods.
Autonomy	Autonomy is the condition of something that does not depend on anything else.
Self-identity	The self-identity is the mental and conceptual awareness and persistent regard that sentient beings hold with regard to their own being.
Intrinsic motivation	Intrinsic motivation causes people to engage in an activity for its own sake. They are subjective factors and include self-determination, curiosity, challenge, effort, and others.
Motivation	In psychology, motivation is the driving force (desire) behind all actions of an organism.
Self-esteem	Self-esteem refers to a person's subjective appraisal of himself or herself as intrinsically positive or negative to some degree.
Chronic	Chronic refers to a relatively long duration, usually more than a few months.
Libido	Sigmund Freud suggested that libido is the instinctual energy or force that can come into conflict with the conventions of civilized behavior. Jung, condidered the libido as the free creative, or psychic, energy an individual has to put toward personal development, or

Go to **Cram101.com** for the Practice Tests for this Chapter.

	individuation.
Acute	Acute means sudden, sharp, and abrupt. Usually short in duration.
Baseline	Measure of a particular behavior or process taken before the introduction of the independent variable or treatment is called the baseline.
Self-awareness	Realization that one's existence and functioning are separate from those of other people and things is called self-awareness.
Sympathetic	The sympathetic nervous system activates what is often termed the "fight or flight response". It is an automatic regulation system, that is, one that operates without the intervention of conscious thought.
Empirical	Empirical means the use of working hypotheses which are capable of being disproved using observation or experiment.
Quantitative	A quantitative property is one that exists in a range of magnitudes, and can therefore be measured. Measurements of any particular quantitative property are expressed as as a specific quantity, referred to as a unit, multiplied by a number.
Affect	A subjective feeling or emotional tone often accompanied by bodily expressions noticeable to others is called affect.
Empathy	Empathy is the recognition and understanding of the states of mind, including beliefs, desires and particularly emotions of others without injecting your own.

Personality	Personality refers to the pattern of enduring characteristics that differentiates a person, the patterns of behaviors that make each individual unique.
Cognitive appraisal	Lazarus' term for individuals' interpretation of events in their lives as threatening, harmful, or challenging and their determination of whether they have the resources to effectively cope with the events is referred to as cognitive appraisal.
Antecedents	In behavior modification, events that typically precede the target response are called antecedents.
Attention	Attention is the cognitive process of selectively concentrating on one thing while ignoring other things. Psychologists have labeled three types of attention: sustained attention, selective attention, and divided attention.
Chronic	Chronic refers to a relatively long duration, usually more than a few months.
Acute	Acute means sudden, sharp, and abrupt. Usually short in duration.
Intrinsic motivation	Intrinsic motivation causes people to engage in an activity for its own sake. They are subjective factors and include self-determination, curiosity, challenge, effort, and others.
Locus of control	The place to which an individual attributes control over the receiving of reinforcers -either inside or outside the self is referred to as locus of control.
Motivation	In psychology, motivation is the driving force (desire) behind all actions of an organism.
Hardiness	A personality characteristic associated with a lower rate of stress-related illness, consisting of three components: commitment, challenge, and control is hardiness.
Anxiety	Anxiety is a complex combination of the feeling of fear, apprehension and worry often accompanied by physical sensations such as palpitations, chest pain and/or shortness of breath.
Trait	An enduring personality characteristic that tends to lead to certain behaviors is called a trait. The term trait also means a genetically inherited feature of an organism.
Affect	A subjective feeling or emotional tone often accompanied by bodily expressions noticeable to others is called affect.
Life satisfaction	A person's attitudes about his or her overall life are referred to as life satisfaction.
Self-esteem	Self-esteem refers to a person's subjective appraisal of himself or herself as intrinsically positive or negative to some degree.
Stress management	Stress management encompasses techniques intended to equip a person with effective coping mechanisms for dealing with psychological stress.
Social support	Social Support is the physical and emotional comfort given by family, friends, co-workers and others. Research has identified three main types of social support: emotional, practical, sharing points of view.
Empirical	Empirical means the use of working hypotheses which are capable of being disproved using observation or experiment.
Individual differences	Individual differences psychology studies the ways in which individual people differ in their behavior. This is distinguished from other aspects of psychology in that although psychology is ostensibly a study of individuals, modern psychologists invariably study groups.
Socioeconomic Status	A family's socioeconomic status is based on family income, parental education level, parental occupation, and social status in the community. Those with high status often have more success in preparing their children for school because they have access to a wide range of

Go to **Cram101.com** for the Practice Tests for this Chapter.

resources.

Socioeconomic	Socioeconomic pertains to the study of the social and economic impacts of any product or service offering, market intervention or other activity on an economy as a whole and on the companies, organization and individuals who are its main economic actors.
Malingering	Malingering is a medical and psychological term that refers to an individual faking the symptoms of mental or physical disorders for a myriad of reasons such as fraud, dereliction of responsibilities, attempting to obtain medications or to lighten criminal sentences.
Perception	Perception is the process of acquiring, interpreting, selecting, and organizing sensory information.
Depression	In everyday language depression refers to any downturn in mood, which may be relatively transitory and perhaps due to something trivial. This is differentiated from Clinical depression which is marked by symptoms that last two weeks or more and are so severe that they interfere with daily living.
Ethnicity	Ethnicity refers to a characteristic based on cultural heritage, nationality characteristics, race, religion, and language.
Attitude	An enduring mental representation of a person, place, or thing that evokes an emotional response and related behavior is called attitude.
Baseline	Measure of a particular behavior or process taken before the introduction of the independent variable or treatment is called the baseline.
Self-efficacy	Self-efficacy is the belief that one has the capabilities to execute the courses of actions required to manage prospective situations.
Self-worth	In psychology, self-esteem or self-worth refers to a person's subjective appraisal of himself or herself as intrinsically positive or negative to some degree.
Questionnaire	A self-report method of data collection or clinical assessment method in which the individual being studied checks off items on a printed list, answers multiple-choice questions, or writes out answers to essay questions aimed at producing a selfdescription is called questionnaire.
Suicide	Suicide behavior is rare in childhood but escalates in adolescence. The suicide rate increases in a linear fashion from adolescence through late adulthood.
Incentive	An incentive is what is expected once a behavior is performed. An incentive acts as a reinforcer.
Theories	Theories are logically self-consistent models or frameworks describing the behavior of a certain natural or social phenomenon. They are broad explanations and predictions concerning phenomena of interest.
Stress inoculation	Use of positive coping statements to control fear and anxiety is a form of stress inoculation.
Guided imagery	Guided imagery is the intentional visualization of images that are calming, relaxing, or beneficial in other ways .
Biofeedback	Biofeedback is the process of measuring and quantifying an aspect of a subject's physiology, analyzing the data, and then feeding back the information to the subject in a form that allows the subject to enact physiological change.
Stages	Stages represent relatively discrete periods of time in which functioning is qualitatively different from functioning at other periods.
Subjective	Subjective experience refers to reality as it is perceived and interpreted, not as it exists

experience	objectively.
Acute pain	Acute pain refers to pain that typically follows an injury and that disappears once the injury heals or is effectively treated.
Trauma	Trauma refers to a severe physical injury or wound to the body caused by an external force, or a psychological shock having a lasting effect on mental life.
Dissociation	Dissociation is a psychological state or condition in which certain thoughts, emotions, sensations, or memories are separated from the rest.
Meditation	Meditation usually refers to a state in which the body is consciously relaxed and the mind is allowed to become calm and focused.
Physiology	The study of the functions and activities of living cells, tissues, and organs and of the physical and chemical phenomena involved is referred to as physiology.
Psychological trauma	Psychological trauma involves a singular experience or enduring event or events that completely overwhelm the individual's ability to cope or integrate the emotion involved with that experience. It usually involves a complete feeling of helplessness in the face of a real or subjective threat to life, bodily integrity, or sanity.
Cognition	The intellectual processes through which information is obtained, transformed, stored, retrieved, and otherwise used is cognition.

Go to **Cram101.com** for the Practice Tests for this Chapter.

Anabolic steroid	Anabolic steroids are a class of natural and synthetic steroid hormones that promote cell growth and division, resulting in growth of muscle tissue and sometimes bone size and strength. Testosterone is the best known natural anabolic steroid, as well as the best known natural androgen.
Steroid	A steroid is a lipid characterized by a carbon skeleton with four fused rings. Different steroids vary in the functional groups attached to these rings. Hundreds of distinct steroids have been identified in plants and animals. Their most important role in most living systems is as hormones.
Growth hormone	Growth hormone is a polypeptide hormone synthesised and secreted by the anterior pituitary gland which stimulates growth and cell reproduction in humans and other vertebrate animals.
Hormone	A hormone is a chemical messenger from one cell (or group of cells) to another. The best known are those produced by endocrine glands, but they are produced by nearly every organ system. The function of hormones is to serve as a signal to the target cells; the action of the hormone is determined by the pattern of secretion and the signal transduction of the receiving tissue.
Brain	The brain controls and coordinates most movement, behavior and homeostatic body functions such as heartbeat, blood pressure, fluid balance and body temperature. Functions of the brain are responsible for cognition, emotion, memory, motor learning and other sorts of learning. The brain is primarily made up of two types of cells: glia and neurons.
Testosterone	Testosterone is a steroid hormone from the androgen group. It is the principal male sex hormone and the "original" anabolic steroid.
Consciousness	The awareness of the sensations, thoughts, and feelings being experienced at a given moment is called consciousness.
Seizure	A seizure is a temporary alteration in brain function expressed as a changed mental state, tonic or clonic movements and various other symptoms. They are due to temporary abnormal electrical activity of a group of brain cells.
Eating disorders	Psychological disorders characterized by distortion of the body image and gross disturbances in eating patterns are called eating disorders.
Testimonial	A testimonial or endorsement is a written or spoken statement, sometimes from a public figure, sometimes from a private citizen, extolling the virtue of some product, which is used in the promotion and advertising of that product.
Protein	A protein is a complex, high-molecular-weight organic compound that consists of amino acids joined by peptide bonds. It is essential to the structure and function of all living cells and viruses. Many are enzymes or subunits of enzymes.
Exogenous	Exogenous refers to an action or object coming from outside a system.
Paranoia	In popular culture, the term paranoia is usually used to describe excessive concern about one's own well-being, sometimes suggesting a person holds persecutory beliefs concerning a threat to themselves or their property and is often linked to a belief in conspiracy theories.
Psychological dependence	Psychological dependence may lead to psychological withdrawal symptoms. Addictions can theoretically form for any rewarding behavior, or as a habitual means to avoid undesired activity, but typically they only do so to a clinical level in individuals who have emotional, social, or psychological dysfunctions, taking the place of normal positive stimuli not otherwise attained
Perception	Perception is the process of acquiring, interpreting, selecting, and organizing sensory information.

Go to **Cram101.com** for the Practice Tests for this Chapter.

Libido	Sigmund Freud suggested that libido is the instinctual energy or force that can come into conflict with the conventions of civilized behavior. Jung, condidered the libido as the free creative, or psychic, energy an individual has to put toward personal development, or individuation.
Guilt	Guilt describes many concepts related to a negative emotion or condition caused by actions which are believed to be, morally wrong. According to Freud, the avoidance of guilt is the basis for moral behavior.
Baseline	Measure of a particular behavior or process taken before the introduction of the independent variable or treatment is called the baseline.
Detoxification	Detoxification in general is the removal of toxic substances from the body. It is one of the functions of the liver and kidneys, but can also be achieved artificially by techniques such as dialysis and (in a very limited number of cases) chelation therapy.
Metabolism	Metabolism is the biochemical modification of chemical compounds in living organisms and cells.
Liver	The liver plays a major role in metabolism and has a number of functions in the body including detoxification, glycogen storage and plasma protein synthesis. It also produces bile, which is important for digestion. The liver converts most carbohydrates, proteing, and fats into glucose.
Central nervous system	The vertebrate central nervous system consists of the brain and spinal cord.
Nervous system	The body's electrochemical communication circuitry, made up of billions of neurons is a nervous system.
Amphetamine	Amphetamine is a synthetic stimulant used to suppress the appetite, control weight, and treat disorders including narcolepsy and ADHD. It is also used recreationally and for performance enhancement.
Stimulant	A stimulant is a drug which increases the activity of the sympathetic nervous system and produces a sense of euphoria or awakeness.
Cocaine	Cocaine is a crystalline tropane alkaloid that is obtained from the leaves of the coca plant. It is a stimulant of the central nervous system and an appetite suppressant, creating what has been described as a euphoric sense of happiness and increased energy.
Barbiturate	A barbiturate is a drug that acts as a central nervous system (CNS) depressant, and by virtue of this produces a wide spectrum of effects, from mild sedation to anesthesia.
Depressant	A depressant is a chemical agent that diminishes a body function or activity. The term is used in particular with regard to the central nervous system where these chemicals are known as neurotransmitters. They tend to act on the CNS by increasing the activity of a particular neurotransmitter known as gamma-aminobutyric acid (GABA).
Depression	In everyday language depression refers to any downturn in mood, which may be relatively transitory and perhaps due to something trivial. This is differentiated from Clinical depression which is marked by symptoms that last two weeks or more and are so severe that they interfere with daily living.
Anxiety	Anxiety is a complex combination of the feeling of fear, apprehension and worry often accompanied by physical sensations such as palpitations, chest pain and/or shortness of breath.
Acute	Acute means sudden, sharp, and abrupt. Usually short in duration.
Stroke	A stroke occurs when the blood supply to a part of the brain is suddenly interrupted by

	occlusion, by hemorrhage, or other causes
Hallucinogen	Certain drugs can affect the subjective qualities of perception, thought or emotion, resulting in altered interpretations of sensory input, alternate states of consciousness, or hallucinations. The term hallucinogen is often broadly applied, especially in current scientific literature, to some or all of these substances.
Amino acid	Amino acid is the basic structural building unit of proteins. They form short polymer chains called peptides or polypeptides which in turn form structures called proteins.
Aerobic exercise	Aerobic exercise is a type of exercise in which muscles draw on oxygen in the blood as well as fats and glucose, that increase cardiovascular endurance.
Anecdotal evidence	Anecdotal evidence is unreliable evidence based on personal experience that has not been empirically tested, and which is often used in an argument as if it had been scientifically or statistically proven. The person using anecdotal evidence may or may not be aware of the fact that, by doing so, they are generalizing.
Conditioning	Conditioning describes the process by which behaviors can be learned or modified through interaction with the environment.
Survey	A method of scientific investigation in which a large sample of people answer questions about their attitudes or behavior is referred to as a survey.
Myocardial infarction	Acute myocardial infarction, commonly known as a heart attack, is a serious, sudden heart condition usually characterized by varying degrees of chest pain or discomfort, weakness, sweating, nausea, vomiting, and arrhythmias, sometimes causing loss of consciousness. It occurs when a part of the heart muscle is injured, and this part may die because of sudden total interruption of blood flow to the area.
Infertility	Infertility is the inability to naturally conceive a child or the inability to carry a pregnancy to term.
Society	The social sciences use the term society to mean a group of people that form a semi-closed (or semi-open) social system, in which most interactions are with other individuals belonging to the group.
Attitude	An enduring mental representation of a person, place, or thing that evokes an emotional response and related behavior is called attitude.
Ego	In Freud's view the Ego serves to balance our primitive needs and our moral beliefs and taboos. Relying on experience, a healthy Ego provides the ability to adapt to reality and interact with the outside world.
Peer pressure	Peer pressure comprises a set of group dynamics whereby a group of people in which one feels comfortable may override the sexual personal habits, individual moral inhibitions or idiosyncratic desires to impose a group norm of attitudes or behaviors.
Locus of control	The place to which an individual attributes control over the receiving of reinforcers -either inside or outside the self is referred to as locus of control.
Rotter	Rotter focused on the application of social learning theory (SLT) to clinical psychology. She introduced the ideas of learning from generalized expectancies of reinforcement and internal/external locus of control (self-initiated change versus change influenced by others). According to Rotter, health outcomes could be improved by the development of a sense of personal control over one's life.
Theory of planned behavior	The theory of planned behavior links attitudes and behavior. It holds that human action is guided by three kinds of considerations: Beliefs about the likely outcomes of the behavior and the evaluations of these outcomes; Beliefs about the normative expectations of others and

Go to **Cram101.com** for the Practice Tests for this Chapter.

	motivation to comply with these expectations; and, Beliefs about the presence of factors that may facilitate or impede performance of the behavior and the perceived power of these factors.
Cognition	The intellectual processes through which information is obtained, transformed, stored, retrieved, and otherwise used is cognition.
Empirical	Empirical means the use of working hypotheses which are capable of being disproved using observation or experiment.
Attention	Attention is the cognitive process of selectively concentrating on one thing while ignoring other things. Psychologists have labeled three types of attention: sustained attention, selective attention, and divided attention.
Self-concept	Self-concept refers to domain-specific evaluations of the self where a domain may be academics, athletics, etc.
Feedback	Feedback refers to information returned to a person about the effects a response has had.
Osteoporosis	Osteoporosis refers to a disorder of aging that involves an extensive loss of bone tissue and is the main reason many older adults walk with a marked stoop. Women are especially vulnerable to osteoporosis.
Amenorrhea	Amenorrhea (AmE) is the absence of a menstrual period in a woman of reproductive age. Physiologic states of amenorrhea are seen during pregnancy and lactation (breastfeeding). Outside of the reproductive years there is absence of menses during childhood and after menopause.
Diagnostic and Statistical Manual of Mental Disorders	The Diagnostic and Statistical Manual of Mental Disorders, published by the American Psychiatric Association, is the handbook used most often in diagnosing mental disorders in the United States and internationally.
Mental disorder	Mental disorder refers to a disturbance in a person's emotions, drives, thought processes, or behavior that involves serious and relatively prolonged distress and/or impairment in ability to function, is not simply a normal response to some event or set of events in the person's environment.
Intrinsic motivation	Intrinsic motivation causes people to engage in an activity for its own sake. They are subjective factors and include self-determination, curiosity, challenge, effort, and others.
Motivation	In psychology, motivation is the driving force (desire) behind all actions of an organism.

Printed in the United Kingdom
by Lightning Source UK Ltd.
121742UK00001BC/27-28/A